BABIES AND TODDLERS FOR MEN

Babies & Toddlers
FOR MEN

From Newborn to Nursery

Mark Woods

Babies and Toddlers for Men: From Newborn to Nursery

This first edition published in 2012 by White Ladder, an imprint of Crimson Publishing Ltd, Westminster House, Kew Road, Richmond, Surrey TW9 2ND.

British Library Cataloguing in Publication Data
A catalogue record for this book is available from the British Library.

ISBN 978 1 90541 091 0

Illustrations by Simon Fitzmaurice

Typeset by IDSUK (DataConnection Ltd)

Printed and bound in the UK by Ashford Colour Press, Gosport, Hants

To Sarah, Stan and little Louis, with all my love

Contents

About the author

Mark Woods has covered national and international stories for the UK's premier news agency, the Press Association; helped to bring a multimillion pound TV company to its knees and is now a writer for the charity Comic Relief.

He lives in south west London with his wife Sarah and sons Stanley and Louis.

Acknowledgements

Thanks and brotherly love to all the fathers who took the time to contribute to this book, your wit and wisdom put my witterings to shame.

Thanks also to the team at Crimson, especially my editor Beth Bishop, who played a huge part in helping to capture three years in 10 chapters, and much gratitude to Rebecca Winfield for the invaluable guiding hand.

Most of all, thank you to my wonderful wife Sarah, not only for the research and re-reading, but also for doing everything else when all I did was write.

INTRODUCTION

Let's not beat about the bush: being a father is the best, most important, most profound thing you'll ever do during your time on the planet.

Yes – you might be a big achiever at work, you might be a formidable competitor on the sports field, or you may even consider yourself pretty special when it comes to sudoku

Laudable and impressive achievements one and all.

But when it comes to making a difference, to leaving your mark during your relatively brief sojourn on our green and pleasant planet, there can be only one show in town. That's your responsibility to – and influence on – the little people you help to bring into being.

As befits something of such magnitude and gravitas, fatherhood comes with a complete working set of highs and lows, triumphs and tragedies, and moments of illumination and despair.

You see, being a father is many things, but anticlimactic isn't one of them.

You can feel intense irritation and impatience before breakfast, frustration and despondency by lunch and an acute sense that you need to earn 37 times more than you do now just after tea.

Threading through all this high emotion will be a sense of fatigue which would be impressive in its tenacity, if it didn't make you feel so utterly wretched.

After the passionate intensity of the conception, the taut anticipation of the pregnancy and the all-round gobsmackingness of the birth, you'd think that with the hard work over you and your partner could settle down to bringing up junior in an idyllic domestic setting.

But even before we join the dad club we are well aware that's garbage.

We've heard the rowing parents in Sainsbury's; we've seen the new dads at work, dragging themselves in like the living dead with a tie on. We've even endured meals while our friends, our once placid and composed friends, have conducted a frantic debate over a nappy full of green poo.

All that and much more will happen to you too – guaranteed.

But it's the things you weren't expecting about parenthood that really take your breath away. Your moments of joy, pride and unbridled love for your little boy or girl go completely unnoticed by the outside world, because they take place in the very deepest part of your chest.

My eldest son saw me coming down the stairs one morning wearing the same blue checked shirt I've been trying to pass off as 'smart' for almost a decade. He looked up and said 'You look nice, Daddy' before skipping off into the kitchen on the hunt for more Marmite on toast.

It doesn't sound much, I know, but it did me all ends up, just like it did the last time he said it. That's not because I knew he'd probably have the last of the Marmite. It's because the minute he and every other child on the planet is born they have their parents in such an emotional half-nelson that at any moment they can render you emotionally incapacitated in quite spectacular fashion.

And that is what's at the heart of all that's great about being a parent in general and a father in particular. No matter how busy, how stressed, or how uptight you might be, you can't fail to have your emotions yanked to the surface at regular intervals. Your child will remind you that you're not only well and truly alive, but that a part of you is alive in someone else now, too.

It's not always lovely, fluffy, gooey emotion that's invoked. When your new-born baby gets her first cold you'll be gripped by a fear the like of which you've yet to experience. She'll snuffle and snort her way through the night, seeming to struggle for each breath.

When your toddler almost wanders out of your momentarily open front door, you will scream like a big girl's blouse before running after them at light speed. Then you will also play the moment over in your head a million times later that night, envisaging the horrors that could have occurred had they taken a few steps more.

Then, when you refuse a request to build the fourth den of the day because you have to check your BlackBerry, you can *taste* the guilt in the roof of your mouth.

And if you lose sight of your little one in a park or shop, even for no more than a second, you will feel every single organ in your body forming orderly queues and preparing to evacuate using both your major orifices.

It's like being possessed.

In a good way.

They don't know or care – they are just kids, playing and being and doing. The only time they will truly know is when they have children of their own and the whole thing will start all over again.

You might not be bitten by this virulent bug straight away, mind you. It may take a little while for evolution to do its thing and turn you into a protector, a provider and a nurturer. But once you are, you are in for life, so you might as well throw yourself at it and enjoy it. You'll *never* feel as important, as worthwhile and as uplifted.

Helping you enjoy your newly found fatherhood is essentially what this book, in its own small way, is trying to do.

There are peaks and troughs aplenty awaiting you over the next few years. Through a combination of research, personal experience (also known as 'mistakes') and speaking to a whole army of new dads I hope to arm you with a decent smattering of information and intelligence on what to expect and what to do when it happens.

The first chapter looks at the time your new little family will spend in hospital before coming home. From then on, each section focusses on a period in your child's life, from the moment she's born to her third birthday.

Sprinkled throughout will be words of wisdom, wonderment and woeful cock-ups from dads who have been there before and lived to tell the tale.

The fact that you are interested enough to read this book means that you want to be a dad who takes an active role in the upbringing of your children. This is a decision that will reward you hugely in the years to come. It can help you to become more empathetic, emotionally literate and even-handed, as you learn from your offspring as much as they learn from you.

Fatherhood can also expose your weaknesses and the more unattractive sides to your personality, and it will certainly tax you physically and mentally in ways you'd not dreamed possible.

That's why we will keep a close eye on how you might be feeling at different stages too, how you're changing as a person and how to begin to get your head around it all.

Not everything that happens in the first three years of your child's life is covered here. But rest assured that the big, juicy, major milestones are all there to for you to read about in one go – or return to when the time is right.

Talking of timing, small children don't give one fig for it. If something is meant to happen in your child's development at a certain time, you and your partner will come to anticipate it, and may get more than a touch vexed if it's late.

'She's not got any teeth yet, why hasn't she got any teeth yet? Next door's baby has teeth, all the babies in the NCT group have teeth, I'm sure mum said I had teeth by now – TEEEEEEEETTTTTHHHH.'

That kind of thing.

So please don't take the timings in this book as a cast iron barometer of exactly when something should sprout or move or change because, unfortunately, uniformity and clockwatching aren't on your tot's agenda whatsoever.

If you are worried about anything to do with your child, seek medical advice as soon as you can. You'll generally find that the entire medical profession display a sense of urgency and focus where treating infants is concerned – in sharp contrast to the nine-hour wait in A&E you are used to after you've stood on the rake again.

There's just one more thing to say before we dive headlong into the first three months – as well as you and your baby or toddler, there's another character in this story and a mightily important one it is too.

Mum, is indeed the word.

Watching the woman you know intimately become a mother before your eyes is in turn a wondrous and disquieting thing. The unbreakable bond they can build with their new baby, the primeval intuition they often discover and the sense of selflessness they demonstrate day after day are humbling phenomena to witness.

These new skills don't come easily (and in some rare cases don't come at all). With more and more women putting burgeoning careers on hold to become mothers, the culture shock alone can take a real toll.

Being a father nowadays is as much about supporting your partner as it is about focussing on your child. So throughout this book you'll come across as much about how your partner is faring as you will about how you are. You'll find a progress report at the end of each chapter that assesses where you and your baby are at during that stage, and what your partner might be experiencing, too.

It's also worth remembering that while supermum is indeed super and while most childcare books are rightly written with her in mind, your often overlooked instincts and nurturing skills are massively important and powerful too.

Study after study has shown that the more involved a father is with his children's upbringing the happier, more stable and even more successful those youngsters become in adolescence and adulthood. Even something as seemingly minor as a father regularly taking part in their children's bathtime has been shown to have a marked impact on emotional health by the time the children reach their teenage years.

No pressure, but you have a huge part to play. To help you on your way, this is a book you can read, refer to and quote in an annoying way during the numerous debates you'll soon be having about how best to bring up your young offspring.

So, let's get cracking.

You live in exciting times my friend, and no matter how it may feel when you are pacing the landing with a screaming infant at 3.37am for the fourth night running, your child will grow up at an alarming rate. Before you know where you are you'll be wistfully reminiscing about babygrows and travel cots – OK, maybe not travel cots – but for now let's move bravely on to what happens immediately after your baby is born.

Don't worry; you're going to be great.

Housekeeping

Babies, as you no doubt know, come in two distinct types. Rather than using the hideous 'he/she' or the impersonal 'they' throughout this book in a bid to try and cover all bases I've decided to only use 'she'.

The reason for this is simple, I went with 'he' in my first book, *Pregnancy for Men*, and it only seems fair.

Also, while I've been annoyingly anal about checking and double checking my research and have also had the whole thing read and approved by consultant paediatrician Dr Jo Jones, this book isn't designed to take the place of professional medical opinion.

But you knew that anyway, didn't you?

Finally, a word on multiple births. Everything in *Babies and Toddlers for Men* is relevant to fathers of twins, triplets and more. But the chances are, if you are the father of multiples you won't have time to read a book for the next decade at least.

I take my hat, coat and odd socks off to all parents who rear more than one baby at a time. How you manage amazes the rest of us, and if this little book helps to make the task ahead of you even a smidgen easier I am very glad indeed.

YEAR 1

WHAT HAPPENS
IN HOSPITAL?

This entire book could be taken up by your first three months of fatherhood.

In fact, this entire book could be taken up by your first three *days* of fatherhood, so powerful can the post-traumatic tidal wave be for all concerned.

You have your partner who, even if she has just performed the most straightforward birth ever recorded in human history, has still undergone physical and emotional upheaval on a quite massive scale.

Having come out the other side of the labour ward she isn't, as feels wholly appropriate, prescribed two weeks of recuperation on a beach, but rather handed a helpless and utterly dependent new-born baby to fathom out and keep alive.

Then there's the little one herself. Imagine for a moment, if you would, what that poor mite has just been through. She's just spent nine months lounging in the amniotic pool, her heavenly life occasionally punctuated by the odd somersault or thumb suck. Then she has, and there's no nice way of saying this, just been forced out of an unfeasibly small hole, or grabbed from above in the most undignified of fashions.

As if the method of her arrival into the world wasn't distressing enough, she's then faced with more bright lights, noise and prodding than her little mind could ever have dreamed existed.

And what about you?

You've tried to do your bit to make life easier through the pregnancy. You've desperately attempted to keep yourself together and be strong through the labour. Now the task in hand is to get to grips with fatherhood and help your new family settle in at home before you are yanked back to work after a few measly weeks.

So all in all, the three of you have had quite a time – and there's a lot you as the proud, excited, but perhaps somewhat daunted father will need to get involved with to make sure these first crucial few weeks and months are navigated as well as possible for your new family.

Before you can get started with family life at home, there will almost certainly be a little (or longer) spell in hospital for your partner and baby to negotiate.

Your part in the recovery

Around 97% of mothers in the UK give birth in hospital.[1] This section focusses on what you can expect to happen in the hours, days, or even in the thankfully rare cases where the baby needs special care, weeks before your new son or daughter can come home.

If your partner has given birth vaginally without complications, she could be back home together with your new baby within hours, at most a couple of days or so.

Given the dire call for beds in most NHS hospitals, the notion that your partner can get some rest and TLC before she is discharged to embark on motherhood is sadly often overridden by the pragmatic need for space.

Having said that, even if there were beds aplenty, your average postnatal ward isn't what you'd call relaxing. The combination of crying newborns, other new mums in turmoil and visiting relatives can combine to make a pretty hectic and unsettling environment and many new mothers can't wait to get home as soon as possible.

In many non-western cultures, once women are at home there often exists a 30 or 40-day 'confinement' – which sounds beastly and patriarchal until you realise that during that time most household activities are carried out by others so the mother and baby can recuperate.

It's also interesting that many cultures overtly and deliberately celebrate *childbirth* rather than the birth of a baby. The mother's role, efforts and well-being are seen on a par with the joy of a new arrival.

While there's tea and sympathy for new mums in our culture, there's no doubting that the star of the show is the bundle of joy in the corner. In many ways, such is the medicalisation of labour it's easy to see how that subtle but important shift happened.

Being there as much as you can for this short but sometimes stressful stay in hospital is a must. Your partner is grappling with a whole world of immediate challenges, including establishing breastfeeding; trying to figure out just when she is meant to rest; wondering what the hell to do with the *Alien*-like umbilical cord stump; or, in many cases, just coming to terms with the reality of being a mother.

Night time can be especially tough and often lonely for your partner after you've been turfed out on your ear at 10pm or so. It's a good idea to keep your mobile on overnight in case she needs to talk. Arriving, cavalry-like, as soon as you're allowed back in the morning will go down well after a tough evening. If you also come armed with something you know she'd love to eat for breakfast you will be a very popular chap indeed. While the NHS can and often does excel on the maternity care front, it's not in any danger of winning a raft of Michelin stars any time soon.

Your partner's postnatal check involves pulse, temperature and blood pressure readings. Her midwife will check that her womb is beginning to contract to its normal size and position. After that, your partner will be able to go home. As long as she has had her first post-birth wee, that is, just to check that all is well with the piping.

If your baby was born by caesarean section, your partner will often stay in hospital for between three to five days all being well. As we will see later, once you get home, you will play a vital role in aiding her recovery from the major surgery she has just endured.

The midwife will want to be sure your partner can walk, albeit gingerly, to the toilet and once there urinate without the need for a catheter, as well as keep food and drink down without vomiting.

Told you it was major surgery.

The baby needs checking out, too, and a paediatrician or a specially trained midwife will carry out a set of remarkably thorough newborn checks before you can take your new family home.

Baby's first check-up

Your baby will be given its first test at just one minute and then again at five minutes after the birth – and you thought setting exams for seven-year-olds was tough.

The Apgar test, devised by the eponymous Dr Virginia Apgar, has been standard practice since the 1950s. The midwife will watch your baby's colour, breathing, behaviour, activity and posture, and then score each of these five factors between zero and two.

A perfect 10 out of 10 is what every new parent wants to hear, but an eight or a nine is still great news. A score between five and seven means your baby is in fair condition but may require some help with breathing. Your midwife may vigorously rub your baby's skin or give her some oxygen if this is the case.

Newborns who score under five are considered to be in poor condition and are often placed on a special unit, which looks a bit like a doner kebab grill, where heat, light and oxygen is on tap to help warm them up and aid breathing. A paediatrician will also be called to help with initial treatment and decide on the best course of action.

The Apgar score is then repeated for babies with low scores, until your baby is in a good and stable condition, or as we will see later, it's decided that treatment in a neonatal ward is a good idea.

Most babies score well, though, and the next job for the midwife is to weigh your baby and measure the circumference of her head. Seven and a half pounds (3.4kg) is seen as the average weight for a newborn these days, although all sorts of factors mean you could have either a petite little thing or a big bouncing bundle of joy that tips the scales above or below that.

This average birth weight has been creeping up for the past 30 years in the UK so that now your average baby boy comes in at 7lb 8oz and girls at 7lb 4oz. The number of babies born weighing more than 9lb 15oz has increased by 20% recently – so be prepared!

Head circumference is a key measurement medically speaking, but it isn't anywhere near as celebrated a birth dimension as weight, is it? If you fancy redressing that balance and sending a text to friends and family reading:

We are delighted to announce the arrival of a baby girl. Mother and daughter doing very well after a tough birth. Olivia Jane is perfect, beautiful and has a head circumference of 34cm.

Do let me know how it goes down.

Then there's the heel prick blood test, usually carried out sometime before your baby is one week old. Although only a tiny amount of blood is taken from the heel, it's a tough one to watch. It goes against every instinct you've got to let someone stick a pin into this delicate and vulnerable little vision of loveliness, but it's for the best, especially when you look at the conditions it is screening for:

> sickle cell disorders

> cystic fibrosis

> medium chain acyl dehydrogenase deficiency(MCADD), a rare condition that affects the way the body converts fat into energy

> phenylketonuria, an enzyme deficiency

> thyroid deficiencies.

The main event, though, is the full newborn examination, a head-to-toe look at your baby that will normally take place between four and 48 hours after birth.

A paediatrician, or midwife with extended training, will check for any health problems or conditions. Ideally you should be there so you can ask questions as it happens, and answer any questions the health professional has about your family's medical history.

Here's a rundown of the main things the examination looks at.

Head

Fear not, some babies often have a strange, almost moulded shape to their head after a vaginal birth caused, as you can imagine, by being squeezed through the birth canal.

Most of these cases will resolve themselves within 48 hours or so. The fontanelles, or soft spots, on your baby's head, which make the whole journey possible for your little one's skull, will also be checked.

If the birth required intervention with either ventouse or forceps, there's also a small risk of your baby's head being bruised or even their neck muscles being damaged, and this will also be looked at.

Mouth

The doctor or midwife will check that the roof of your baby's mouth is complete. If a cleft palate is detected, it will need surgery and could well make feeding difficult.

Eyes

The doctor or midwife will shine a light from an ophthalmoscope into your baby's eyes to look for a red reflex, the same red reflex that ruins many a photo. In this case, red eye is a very good thing indeed as it means cataracts or other rare conditions can be ruled out.

Heart

Your baby's heart will be listened to for heart murmurs or any other sounds that shouldn't be there. Murmurs are not uncommon in these early days – your baby's circulation goes through some pretty major changes as it adjusts to life without the umbilical cord. Heart murmurs often require a second opinion and further investigation, but they often disappear on their own.

Genitals

Your baby's genitals can often give you a bit of a fright when you first see them after birth. Sometimes swollen or a dark angry colour, or even both, this is down to the maternal hormones your baby was exposed to before the big arrival.

These are the same hormones which could also cause your baby to have engorged breasts, regardless of gender and for girls to have a clear or even slightly bloody vaginal discharge for the first few weeks.

In boys, the scrotum is checked for undescended testes and his penis will be checked to ensure the opening is at the tip and not on the underside, which would cause all sorts of problems, as you can imagine.

Lungs

Your baby's breathing pattern will be observed and his lungs will be listened to with a stethoscope to ensure there is a clear equal entry of air into them both.

Skin

Your baby's skin will be checked for all manner of exotic sounding birthmarks, including stork marks, strawberry marks and Mongolian spots.

Hands and feet

As you'd expect, fingers and toes are counted and the feet are checked for webbing (around one baby in every 2,000 is born with two or more toes fused together).

The resting position of your baby's feet and ankles will also be checked for club foot, which is where the front half of the foot turns in and down.

Hips

Your baby's hips will be given a good old to and fro to check the stability of the joints. Most NHS trusts routinely scan hips these days, too. If any instability or clicks are picked up, further tests will be carried out.

Reflexes

Your baby's reflexes are truly a thing of wonder. The innate ability to suck that most babies possess at birth is impressive in itself, but the rooting reflex, nature's way of helping the most helpless of tots find their food, is nothing short of amazing. Gently brush one of your new-born baby's cheeks and chances are she will instinctively turn her head to that side on the hunt for milk.

Then there's the grasp reflex. So strong is it that many newborns can cling on to your fingers and support their own weight – not that it's advisable to try this out!

Why a seemingly frail and needy little newborn should be able to perform this extraordinary gymnastic feat is even more astonishing than the act itself. Anthropologist Desmond Morris explains[2] that the ability to cling on with such intensity is a reminder of our close evolutionary ties to the monkeys and apes, whose young grasp their mother's fur for all their worth from the get-go, as they are transported through the tree canopy.

Most modern mums give the Tarzan routine a miss nowadays, so this initial reflex soon fades, but when your finger is grasped by a tiny hand you'll be witnessing many thousands of years of evolutionary history.

The examiner will test that all of these reflexes are functioning properly and will also carry out the Moro test. This entails holding your baby face up with one hand under its bottom and one holding its head. The hand holding the head is allowed to drop by a few centimetres. The Moro reflex should then kick in and your baby will fling out both her legs and arms with fingers spread. The examiner is looking for symmetry here.

Your baby will probably cry for a little while after this, which is perfectly understandable.

Ears

Many hospitals now give babies a hearing test before you are discharged from hospital. This is often carried out by a specialist nurse or midwife who brings two very special bits of kit to your partner's bedside.

The first test is called otoacoustic emissions (OAEs). A miniature earphone and microphone are placed in the ear, sounds are played and if the baby hears normally, an echo is reflected back into the ear canal and is measured by the microphone.

The second test is the auditory brainstem response or ABR, in which electrodes are placed on the baby's head (it's nowhere near as bad as it sounds) to detect brain responses from sounds played via earphones.

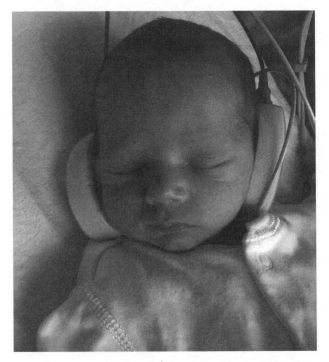

Even at this tender age they know how to use an iPod.

So as you can see, your newborn will be given a pretty rigorous check-up in her first few days. If, as most babies do, she passes her first ever set of exams with flying colours, you'll be relieved and proud in equal measure.

But things don't always go to plan where delicate new lives are concerned. Between 6%–10% of babies spend some time in a neonatal or special care unit through ill health, premature birth or because they need special monitoring (for example, if the mother was diabetic).

Special care in a special place

There are many reasons why your baby could be admitted to the neonatal ward – including being born prematurely, underweight or because of a range of illnesses or conditions, including any maternal conditions that may have affected the baby.

Although the circumstances may vary, what's true in every case is the utter shock that you as parents feel watching your son or daughter struggle.

When our youngest son was born unexpectedly six weeks early, we spent almost a month helplessly watching as he fought off severe jaundice. He was fed via a tube into his tiny stomach while he slowly learnt the sucking reflex he'd not had time to perfect in the womb.

Compared with many of the other children in the unit he was a big healthy boy at four pounds – odd and he had no conditions that required surgery. But to us it was the most intense and initially bewildering period in our entire lives.

We sat for hour after hour peering into the incubator, listening to the beeps of the monitors plugged into our boy. The sight of another couple on the ward getting ready to take their baby home filled us with hope and a desperate longing to be able to do the same.

As the days passed, and we got to know and talk to the staff as they expertly went about their business, we begun to realise how lucky we were. Neonatal nurses and doctors are the crème de la crème. While in the labour ward, it's sometimes the case that dads are treated, or at least can be made to feel, like a spare part, I never felt this once in the neonatal unit. Every dad I spoke to during my time there said the same.

There are usually three different levels of care on neonatal units depending on your baby's needs.

1. **Intensive care** (neonatal intensive care, or NICU), for the most gravely ill or premature babies.

2. **High dependency** (HD) care, for babies who are not on the critical list but who still need complex care.

3. **Special care** (SC), for otherwise well babies who are catching up on growth and development after a premature birth, or those who are getting better after more complex treatment.

Some babies move through these levels as they improve, or heartbreakingly back again if they regress.

Most neonatal units are open 24 hours a day for parents to visit. When you can't be at the hospital – or when you wake up in the morning at home after a fitful night's sleep and the memory of what is happening floods back – you can call the nursery and talk directly to the nurse who is caring for your baby.

Remember that just because there's a high level of medical care being delivered, you and your partner still know your baby best and your instincts are to be trusted. In my experience, the staff recognise and encourage this and treat you as part of the team.

There are many ways you can help your baby, such as getting involved in the feeding, even if this is via tube. Most wards have breast pumps and cold storage space so that new mums can express milk so that even if the baby can't suckle yet, they are still getting their mother's milk and all the benefits that brings.

You can also do all of the usual baby care duties like washing and changing them if your baby is strong enough. If your baby is small, this will take some getting used to, especially for first time parents, but the staff generally have infinite patience and expertise and will guide you through.

'Kangaroo care' is also something that not just benefits your baby, but also does you the power of good. It's nothing complex, but the results have been proved to be remarkable. You simply hold your nappy-only baby inside your shirt upright against your bare skin with her head turned so her ear is above your heart. The technique, pioneered in the mid-80s in Bogotá, Columbia, was devised because of the lack of reliable power and equipment available – almost immediately the mortality rate fell from 70% to 30%.

The most important thing you can do is to look after yourself and – crucially – your partner during this tough time. Leaving a baby in hospital after she has been discharged is perhaps one of the most painful and unnatural of experiences a mother can have. You need to be there to help her come through it, despite the worry and angst you are feeling yourself.

What's for certain is that if your newborn has to spend time in neonatal, they could not be in better hands.

In a strange way we left the ward feeling that in an ideal, budget-no-issue world, this is the kind of post-birth care everyone would receive. Not the incubators and the feeding tubes, but the one-to-one care; the staff with the time and expertise to reassure and educate; and the sense that when you depart, you do so with real confidence that you and your child have been looked after to an exceptionally high standard.

Words from your fellow fathers

Ben, father of two: *The care my wife and baby received was amazing on both occasions.*

We had our first at a hospital with a doctor on call as we were worried about complications. However, after the baby was born we then transferred to a midwife-led unit at our nearest hospital. It was like a baby hotel and the staff were incredible. It was very relaxed and there was plenty of time for the midwives to help my wife learn how to bath the baby, feed, etc. They even took him for a couple of hours to make sure she got some sleep.

We had our second at the midwife-led unit and they all remembered my wife and this made her feel at ease during the birth. Five-star service.

Nick, father of two: *Evenings were quite lonely for my wife and a more brutal nurse type tends to be on duty.*

My wife spent the days complaining that her new first born was ginger – my fault due to an unrevealed gene that had crept in a few generations back. She was quite vocal about it until the curtain around the bed next door was pulled back and revealed a young family together with close relations, all of whom were about as ginger as it gets.

In the end I upgraded her to a private room. Money well spent – comfortable, quiet and relaxed. Only disturbed once or twice by the delivery of Bounty baby bags made up of baby brands like Pampers, nappy rash creams and – scarily –Red Bull (someone knew what I was in for).

A man came in and asked if we would like a family photo for £10. I then realised what a baby factory I was in, complete with cross-sell and up-sell opportunities.

Stuart, father of two: *Our hospital experience was pretty good all round except being turfed out at four in the morning after my partner had been in labour for over 27 hours.*

Leaving her alone to fend for this new little person that we'd made together made me feel sad looking back, but at the time I was still shell-shocked that it was all for real.

I was allowed back at about 8ish, so for the sake of a few hours you'd think they would have let me stay?

Your progress report

Your baby

Life outside the womb must be pretty bewildering in these first few days for the new-born baby. Understandably, they spend much of their time becoming accustomed to the light, noise and amount of space they have to unfurl their scrunched-up limbs.

Your newborn's vision is pretty blurry at this stage. She can only see well up to about 45cm/18in away – which, as it cleverly happens, is about the distance from the breast to the mother's face– so keep close to her whenever she's alert

Her specialist subject is the face for this early spell and you'll catch her staring you down at any given opportunity. This intent study is her way of memorising your features so she can recognise the people who are legally responsible for her welfare should any litigation be required at a later date.

While it's a strict diet of milk at this stage, your baby's taste buds can already distinguish between sweet and sour flavours, so she can tell the difference between fresh and gone-off versions of the white stuff.

Other than perfecting face recognition technology and establishing a burgeoning career as a milk tester, she will also be weeing up to 18 times a day and pooing anything between four and seven times daily. As long as she is having at least one bowel movement a day things are probably OK in that department. A single 24-hour span without a poo isn't cause for panic as long as the nappies continue to be wet, but any longer than that and it's time to seek medical advice. Your baby should poo within 24 hours of birth.

In terms of colour and consistency, in the early days, a newborn's poo tends to be thick and dark green in colour. This first

proto-poop is called meconium – which is so sticky and seemingly indestructible that it could be the answer to the pothole problems that blight our roads.

As your baby starts to feed properly you will be confronted, on opening the nappy, by yellowish matter which has more than a passing resemblance to chicken korma. It is usual for your baby's poo to vary in colour each day depending – if she is breastfeeding – on what your partner has been eating.

Your partner

If all has gone well, your partner will be beyond relieved that your baby is healthy and that she herself has managed to get through the labour, which has hung over her like the sword of Damocles for nine months.

As we will see in the next chapter, there's an awful lot of physical recovering to be done. But for now the sense of post-birth achievement, pride and love mixes in nicely with exhaustion and a healthy shot of anxiety and apprehension at how she will perform as a mum. As far as I can tell, this cocktail is ever present throughout parenthood to a greater or lesser degree.

Being in hospital is rarely a joy, no matter what the circumstances, so being there to make life even a modicum better for her is a must. Speaking to the staff, taking charge of your baby so she can go for a tentative wander, bringing in her favourite food, whatever it takes, she'll really appreciate it.

As if she needed any added pain, it's normal for your partner to be constipated for at least a couple of days after having the baby. She's had high levels of the hormone progesterone in her body during pregnancy, and her digestive system has almost shut down completely during labour as all available resources were mustered for the main job in hand. It may well be a while before normal service is resumed.

If she's anxious about the first time she does do a 'number two', try and reassure her about it and suggest she tries to take her mind off it by reading a magazine. She doesn't need to make life harder than it already is by being tense in the vital area. If she's had a C-section, she might have been given a mild laxative to make things a bit easier.

Welcome to your new world!

You

There's something magical about the few days between when your first baby is born and when mother and child finally arrive home.

I remember prancing around about like Norman Wisdom after my eldest was born. I floated into the florist to get my wife some flowers and told the kindly woman who ran the place just how beautiful my son was and how in awe of his mother I felt, like I was the very first new father to have happened across her shop. (I didn't know that the flowers would end up on the nurses' desk because they were banned from the ward for hygiene reasons.)

That's how you feel – yes you know that during the time it's taken you to choose between fuchsias and roses another 20 infants have been born elsewhere on the planet, but it matters not – you feel elated and proud and special and why not?

You are.

Milk it and enjoy every minute. If you have a second it will still be amazing but because you'll have another youngster in need of some care and attention back home you won't be able to give it the Mr Grimsdale impression in quite the same way.

MONTHS 0-3

The first day of the rest of your life

The time has come to take your new family home and begin your life as a father.

From the moment you check for the ninth time that the car seat is secured properly before you drive away from the hospital, you will feel the weight of responsibility and nervousness wrestling with the giddiness of excitement and pride inside your overcrowded head.

It may be a cliché, but when your front door closes behind you, the chances are you and your partner will glance at each other in time-honoured fashion and wonder – what now?

The answer will soon become very apparent.

This first intense three-month spell is about one thing: getting to know the little person who has just moved in to your home. Getting to know how she feeds, how she reacts, how she sleeps (good luck with that one!) – getting to know who and how she is.

You should have at least two weeks' paternity leave (the generosity of it!) so you can explore and enjoy the new arrival with your partner as you both begin the ever-evolving process of finding out how you will parent your child.

Perhaps the most fundamental of all the areas you'll be tackling as a couple will be how to keep your milk-obsessed baby well fed. As we will see in detail, fundamental it may be, straightforward it most certainly isn't.

A very close cousin of the M word is the T word – *thrive*. Your baby's growth, general health and toilet habits will become your household's new fixation. Forget the football, forget the holidays, forget the extension to the kitchen you've always talked about; percentile points, Sudocrem and mastitis will be the new idiom at your place.

Like the earliest people on the planet, you now live in a world of firsts; the first bath, the first cry you can't calm, the first smile – they just keep on coming. Each one represents a challenge or a moment of joy (often at the same time) that will grab your undivided attention in a way you would not believe.

Your partner, as well as facing the biggest challenge of her life, is also recovering from the kind of physical and hormonal kicking that only women have the fortitude to withstand once, let alone a number of times.

'Baby blues', a term so weak and patronising that it should be booted from the baby lexicon for good, can and often does strike. The more you know about it ahead of time, the more you'll be able to help. It's bigger and altogether more serious brother, postnatal depression, is also something you need to be clued up on.

And don't think you're immune, either.

This first three months may sound daunting, and I won't lie to you, it is, but you'll get through it. What's more, I hope that amid all the nappies and the night feeds you'll be able to find fleeting moments when you can breathe in the magnitude and magnificence of what you are doing.

And you can help your partner take time away from the coalface to do the same.

I promise you'll be through this stage before you know where you are and you'll probably even begin to miss it.

It just doesn't feel like it's ever going to end at the time, that's all.

Feeding your baby

I remember thinking as I skipped into hospital swinging an empty car seat to and fro (Norman Wisdom again) that in half an hour's time or so everything would be different.

There's no other moment in your life when you will be entrusted with something so delicate, fragile and precious as when you collect your baby and head for home.

Once you've had the obligatory GULP! moment when reality dawns that the pair of you need to immediately transform from looking after yourselves pretty badly, to taking care of someone else fantastically well, stuff begins to happen.

For your baby this isn't a particularly momentous occasion. This is just the next moment on her unstoppable march towards growth and development. In the first few weeks a huge driver of those twin objectives is eating.

There's very little that's as fundamental or as emotive for you and your partner in the first few months of parenthood as the process of feeding your baby.

You'd think it would be a doddle – what could be more straightforward? The hungry little one can either take sustenance from the two ready-made milk dispensers that your partner has cleverly developed, or if for whatever reason that doesn't appeal, formula milk is a tried and tested alternative that works perfectly well for millions.

Job done, let's move on, time to start worrying about university tuition fees.

Not quite.

For many, many mothers breastfeeding is incredibly hard. It can be excruciatingly painful. Given that the breast has yet to evolve into an opaque container with clearly defined ounce markings it can also be very hard to know, especially in the crucial first few weeks, when and if your baby has had her fill.

Then there's the stigma, guilt and even shame around the whole area of 'breastfeeding failure' which many new mothers feel when things don't go to plan.

You have a big part to play here, not just as chief bottle washer if that's the route you end up taking, but also in supporting your partner through what can be a highly emotional and devilishly difficult time.

To do that you'll need to understand some of the details at the heart of the breast vs bottle debate.

Breastfeeding

Barely a week goes by, it seems, without a new study reinforcing that breast is best on all sorts of levels.

As well as providing the most nutritious food for newborns and infants, breastmilk contains antibodies that help protect against a host of childhood illnesses and chronic diseases. It has also been claimed that breastfeeding can reduce the incidence of childhood obesity.

According to studies, infants who are breastfed also have lower risk of gastroenteritis, respiratory tract infections, childhood leukemia, asthma, allergies, diabetes, heart disease, hypertension, cot death – the list just keeps on growing.

Even the act of breastfeeding appears to be capable of developing proper jaw and teeth alignment in your child. Some studies have also indicated that breastfed babies have slightly higher intelligence quotients (IQs) than those who are bottlefed.

A study published in May 2011[3] even found that children who are breastfed for four months or more develop fewer behaviour problems in later life. This is believed to be due to the make-up of the milk itself and/or the better mother/baby interaction that breastfeeding fosters.

It doesn't stop there – mothers also benefit. Breastfeeding mums burn more calories and can drop pre-pregnancy weight more quickly and according to research they even have decreased risks of postnatal depression, type 2 diabetes, breast and ovarian cancers, and bone density problems.

The US Department of Health[4] even goes as far to say that the American nation benefits when mothers breastfeed. It explains that if 90% of US newborns were breastfed exclusively for six months, the US would save $13 billion per year because medical care costs are lower for fully breastfed infants.

Just in case the message hasn't hit home hard enough, Uncle Sam also lobs in that breastfeeding contributes to a more productive national workforce because mothers miss less work to care for sick infants.

And – oh yeah – it'll also help save the planet because it produces less waste.

No pressure then.

A lot of that impressive body of evidence is common sense. Breastmilk is a dynamic fluid that changes throughout your baby's life. It's the food nature intended them to have and it's available without the need for spending money on formula and discarding the empties.

As ever, it seems that there's another argument to listen to. In 2009 Michael Kramer, a professor of paediatrics who has advised the World Health Organization and UNICEF (the United Nations Children's Fund) claimed that much of the evidence used to persuade mothers to breastfeed was either wrong or out of date.

He observed that because mothers who breastfed were often more likely to follow advice on all health issues in general, their conscientious approach was more likely to explain a lot of the benefits attributed to breastmilk, rather than the miraculous substance itself.

While he said that some of the claims were well-founded, he added that:

> *'The formula milk industry jumps on every piece of equivocal evidence. But the breastfeeding lobby have a way of ignoring the evidence. Both sides are not being very scientific.'[5]*

Despite some doubts over the degrees involved, it does seem pretty clear and in many ways logical that breast is indeed best for the baby – but is it always an achievable or even desirable goal for the mother? The answer is no. Many new mums find the mechanics of breastfeeding impossible or that simply making a choice right from the off isn't for them.

While what's been called the 'breastmilk mafia' has a habit of sneering somewhat on those that make the latter call, it's crucial your partner feels you back her to the hilt, whatever she decides.

The elusive 'latch'

The Department of Health's recommendation for feeding infants is that exclusive breastfeeding for the first six months is the best approach.

The Department's own Infant Feeding Survey painted a picture of a reality in sharp contrast with that ideal.

While 76% of mothers said that they wanted to breastfeed at the very start of their pregnancy (this number had encouragingly risen to 80% in the preliminary findings of a 2010 study), just one week in, the number exclusively doing so was down to 45%.

By six weeks the figure had dropped to 21% and at the four-month mark just 7% of babies still had breastmilk as their sole sustenance.

By six months the figure was, in the words of the survey,'negligible'.

When you consider the same survey found that eight in every 10 mums said they *were* aware of the health benefits of breastfeeding it does beg the question: What the hell's going on?

The answer seems to be that while women are encouraged to start breastfeeding by the state and the medical profession, the support that many new mums need to become comfortable and confident with breastfeeding isn't there for long enough. So they move on to bottlefeeding. One study showed that two-thirds of midwives interviewed did not even discuss formula feeding with new parents.

The trouble is that breastfeeding, despite being as natural a bodily function as sneezing, is a fiendishly delicate thing to perfect, with the latch at the heart of it all.

If your baby isn't connecting with your partner's nipple in the right way (there are a plethora of videos on YouTube showing the 'correct' latch if you want to see for yourself – I'd be careful watching them at work mind you) it can cause the devil's own trouble with cracked, painful or even bleeding nipples rendering the whole process a nightmare.

While you can't guarantee a pain-free breastfeeding experience for your partner, you can make a tangible day-to-day difference when she is attempting to make it work. Breastfeeding seems to bring on an instantaneous killer thirst and major hunger pangs. So: Is she comfortable, does she have a drink and a snack to hand and has she got somewhere warm and quiet to focus on the task in hand?

Even with all the environmental touches in place things can still be tough and painful. Mastitis, when the breast tissue becomes inflamed and then often infected due to milk build-up, is also an all-too-common occurrence. It can lead to a thoroughly miserable time for your poor partner.

And the physical pain often isn't even the worst of it. What adds to the pressure is that while each feed seems to become more of a disaster to the increasingly fraught mum, you are both faced with a new-born baby who needs to be fed.

The logical response in this situation is to express some milk and bottlefeed it while still trying to get the hang of the breast technique. Or, if expressing is too painful, use bottlefed formula to buy some time to get things right.

Logical but very controversial – welcome to the 'nipple confusion' debate.

This hot issue centres around advice often given in recent years that if your baby so much as looks at a bottle teat they will reject the real deal out of hand.

The thinking being that the bottle offers up a reservoir of milk so easy to get at that your canny baby will simply cock a snook at Mother Nature's finest from that moment onwards. (By the way, both shaking your head for no and sticking your tongue out for displeasure are believed to be derived from ways that babys tell you they've had enough milk.)

This line of thinking is slowly being debunked and the pressure on new mums to perfect breastfeeding within the first few days, without having the safety net of the bottle to see them through, is gradually being lifted.

Clare Byam-Cook, a leading feeding specialist, is particularly vigorous in putting the boot into the nipple/teat naysayers in her book *What to Expect When You're Breastfeeding. . .And What if You Can't?* giving realistic and pragmatic advice to mums.

Technique is at the heart of many a breastfeeding problem and conflicting or misinformation abounds from midwives, health visitors, friends and even parents. So doing some research ahead of time and calling in help when things are tough will pay dividends.

The first few days after birth are crucial for breastfeeding success. The super-rich, super-powerful colostrum is up for grabs before your partner's milk is 'let down', but statistics show that, the drop-off is a very steep one after that first week.

If your partner needs help with her technique in those first few days, don't be shy in getting on the phone (with her consent) and talking to community midwives. Ideally, ask a breastfeeding specialist, if there's one in the area, to come round and help out. Or there's the National Childbirth Trust breastfeeding helpline on 0300 330 0771 and the NHS national breastfeeding helpline on 0300 100 0212 – both of which can hook you up with a specialist breastfeeding counsellor quickly.

If you don't ask, you won't get, and it can make all the difference.

Quantity

Another issue that can kick breastfeeding into the long grass is the fact that you never really know just how much milk your baby has had – and there's no conclusive way of finding out.

There are signs you can look out for, which – while not being as decisive as an empty bottle – at least give you both a clue how things are going.

If your baby is feeding at least six to eight times a day that's a very good sign. So is the fact that the act of breastfeeding is painless for your partner.

While the feed is taking place, your baby should be noticeably swallowing and changing her rhythm of sucking and even pausing during the feed to take a breather. Wet nappies are another key indicator – once she's past five days old or so your baby should have at least six to eight wet nappies every 24 hours, and the wee itself should also be pale and relatively odorless.

Your baby's poo should be a yellowy mustard colour if feeding is firing on all cylinders. Looking at the Dulux colour chart, you're after a deposit giving off a 'sunflower symphony'-type glow. And your partner should sense that her breasts feel emptier and softer after a good feed, too.

So you can see there's a lot going on for the new mother in your house. If things take a turn for the worst early on it really can reduce the first few weeks of motherhood to a guilt-ridden carnival of cracked nipples and crying.

Not good.

Your support, love and understanding are crucial. The social and moral pressure that some mums feel to succeed as they put themselves through hell can be overwhelming. Knowing that you support her whatever the outcome will go a long way to giving her the belief to either carry on trying or to make the switch to formula. She can feel safe in the knowledge that it is a joint decision free from shame, blame or judgement.

Bottlefeeding

If, for whatever reason, you decided to go down the formula route, rather than being the social pariahs you may consider yourselves, the figures, as we have seen, show you are in the majority. So give yourselves a break and crack on.

There are father-specific benefits to bottlefeeding. You can help share the burden and take the strain of some of the feeds, especially the night time ones.

Yeah! (More enthusiasm needed please.)

What is unequivocally joysome is the fact that you get to share in the closeness and serenity of looking into your baby's eyes as you help them grow and thrive. It's a very lovely thing feeding your baby and while down the line you'll no doubt have your phone on the arm of the sofa, the TV on silent and a paper balanced on your feet, it's worth, for these first few months at least, finding a peaceful spot and lapping up every moment of your babe in arms. She will be a running, jumping, talking little person very soon indeed.

Not that bottlefeeding is a breeze. You've got to sterilise the equipment, make up the bottle in the correct way and give your baby said bottle while causing as little wind and vomit as possible. You can manage all that, though, you're a dad now.

If you notice any lingering guilt your partner may be feeling about bottlefeeding do your level best to expel it. Your lives as parents are full of decisions and choices you'll need to make that affect your child, and this is just one of them.

If your baby is content, enjoying every drop of their bottles and vitally, as we are about to see, thriving, then just count your blessings and enjoy.

Thriving

No matter how you decide to feed your baby you will become obsessed, consumed and just a little boring to almost everyone else on the planet about how your little one is progressing on her growth chart in her first few weeks and months.

Most babies lose some weight in the first two weeks of life as they shed the extra fluid they are born with. A healthy newborn is expected to lose 7%–10% of their birth weight but should regain that weight by about two weeks after birth. During their first month, most newborns continue to gain weight at a rate of at least five ounces (141g) a week. Many newborns go through a period of rapid growth when they are 7–10 days old and again at three and six weeks.

If your baby was born significantly prematurely, your health professionals will use what's called her corrected age, taking account of her early birth date, when they mark her progress on the chart.

Many factors determine how heavy or tall your baby will be. If and when you are told that your little beauty is on the 11th percentile for weight – essentially meaning that 89% of other babies her age weigh more, try and curb any competitive, 'there must be some mistake, do the calculation again, do it again I tell you!' outbursts.

It's fine.

What matters is that your baby sticks pretty much to that line as she grows. Whether she is on the 1st, 50th or 100th mark doesn't really matter. What quickly becomes important is that she doesn't consistently dip below where she should be. If she does, there's a chance you could hear the words 'failure to thrive' mentioned by a doctor or health visitor. Some babies gradually slide up or down the centiles over the first year. This is usually normal, and called 'catch up' or 'catch down' growth and is due to genetic factors kicking in.

Failure to thrive

It's hard to think of a more dread-laden phrase. It's immediately terrifying and has the potential to extract more fluid from your guilt glands than anything you've ever heard before in your entire life. All it really means is that your baby is growing more slowly than other children of the same age.

There's no real agreed definition for the term. The diagnosis usually comes about directly from the lack of the required progress over a period of time as shown on the growth chart, rather than from any specific physical signs.

If you find yourself having to deal with this situation, don't let guilt dominate your thoughts. The problem may well be easy to put right and feeling guilty isn't going to help make that happen.

What will get things back on track is working with your health visitor or doctor to find the cause. As part of that process, they may well watch your partner breastfeed or you both bottlefeed your baby, to see if there are any obvious issues with the amount of milk your baby is getting.

Sometimes the problem can be caused by an allergy or intestinal problems. In very rare cases it can indicate a more serious underlying problem – and it goes without saying that the earlier anything like that is spotted the better.

....

Words from your fellow fathers

Murray, father of two: *I remember a general feeling when we first got home that I/we weren't competent enough to look after such a small thing that relied on us totally.*

You realise that in time that instinct is generally right – this is what you are meant to do.

Mark, father of one: *My wife tried breastfeeding for the first month and she didn't really get on with it, she found it painful and we had a hungry baby on our hands!*

She tried expressing which helped but we didn't last long. There was not much I could do other than be supportive of what she wanted. She was trying her best and it was all new and daunting so no point creating more stress than we needed, particularly when there seem to be so many good alternatives.

Colin, father of two: *Breastfeeding was a nightmare to begin with. My wife suffered terrible cracked nipples, bleeding, infections, the lot. To her credit, though, she pushed through and ended up feeding for seven months.*

I felt so helpless during the tough times – the hardest thing was not knowing how much milk baby was getting and how much is left in the boob. If only there was a gauge to let you know how much is left. Maybe someone will design an app for that!

Steve, father of two: *I actively encouraged my wife to breastfeed for as long as possible. . .it's amazing for the baby, you've got to persevere.'*

Some argued that my enthusiasm was partly because it meant she always had to get up with the baby when she cried for food and I didn't have to – and in hindsight they probably had a point.

I remember thinking so clearly after a while that maybe we needed to go to bottles when my wife had reached a level of exhaustion which is difficult to articulate. She was trying to feed our daughter in bed but kept falling asleep. Olivia was inches away from the breast dripping in milk, but could not quite reach it.

This wake-up call for me meant that from then on we used the bottle and our daughter got stronger faster and as a result slept more – resulting in more sleep for ourselves.

I learnt to not be so selfish with our second child, although my wife had heard all of my lines before and would never have fallen for them the second time round anyway!

Nick, father of two: *My wife didn't enjoy the breastfeeding experience. She found it really painful.*

The other challenge was pumping. It becomes quite clear that pumping unused milk was essential. We went for a double pump (we're those kind of people – a double pump family). I was in charge of trying to get the pump to work. Reading the German instructions, at 2am, crouched on the landing in just my boxer shorts, was a low point.

The S word: Part 1

Sleep is going to become your new obsession.

Your sleep, your baby's sleep, your partner's sleep – you'll come to think about them all an awful lot.

In fact, it could keep you awake at night, if you were getting any sleep to interrupt, that is.

Rather than trying to re-establish a 'normal' sleeping regime in your household it's best, for these first few weeks at least, to just accept it.

Accept that you will be tired, accept that you will be beyond tired and accept that despite it all, you'll just have to carry on. Think of it not as something to be endured but as a rite of passage, an extreme sport to be taken on and beaten.

With that in mind, let's leave the tips and techniques for later when your baby is ready to play ball.

Sleep: the facts

New-born babies sleep a lot – up to 18 hours a day for the first few weeks and 15 hours a day by three months.

Sounds great, what's all the fuss about? Thing is, she'll probably never sleep for more than three or four hours at a time, day or night.

Killer that it is, this is a crucial phase for your baby. These short sleep cycles mean she will spend more time in rapid eye movement (REM) sleep, allowing her brain to carry out the truly remarkable changes it needs to.

The phenomenal transformation you'll witness in your child over her first year, from her behaviour, understanding, and interaction is driven by a period of brain development and activity which puts us adults to shame.

Interestingly, boys' and girl's brains develop differently in a very physical sense. A boy's brain develops from the back – the doing part – towards the front – the thinking part – whereas a girl's brain develops in the opposite direction. What that means is that boys develop their physical abilities before they start to think about them.

Sounds familiar.

Whereas girls develop more of their thinking and language skills first, which helps to explain why girls seem to race ahead when the time for school comes around.

In some small way the knowledge that your disturbed sleep is helping your baby to think for herself might help you feel a bit less cranky as you walk up and down the landing for the third time that night – not *that* much less, mind you.

Things change quickly. At six to eight weeks, most babies begin to sleep for shorter spells during the day and longer periods at night, although most continue to wake up for at least one feed.

It is possible, apparently, for some babies to sleep through the night when they are as young as eight weeks old, but it's the exception to the rule. It won't feel like that when seemingly every other couple you know is claiming to have a 'go-through-the-nighter' from about day four. They are liars, liars I tell you! In all probability your little one will be up at night for at least the first few months or often much later than that.

Sorry.

There is a whole world of techniques, methods and philosophies for getting your baby to sleep. We shall wade into the sodden fields of the 'baby wars', as the fierce debate around them has been dubbed, in the next chapter.

For now, let's look at one area of the sleep arena that has claimed thousands of utterly tragic casualties over the years, but which finally seems to be on the retreat – cot death.

Cot death

If miscarriage is the spectre that haunts early pregnancy, then cot death is the dark cloud hanging over the new parent.

Cot death, also known as SIDS – sudden infant death syndrome – isn't an illness but a diagnosis given when an apparently healthy baby dies without warning.

There are around 300 cot deaths in the UK each year – a number which represents a 70% fall since the introduction of the *Reduce the Risk* campaign in 1991. At the heart of this campaign was the message that putting your baby to sleep on its front was a contributory factor in cot death.

Since then, 'Back to Sleep' has become a watch word in baby care and taking the simple measure of putting your little one to sleep on their back is proving to be a key factor in winning the battle over this truly petrifying phenomenon.

But despite the success of the past 20 years, no one knows for sure why SIDS happens. Ongoing research points to a number of potential factors at play. They include the suggestion that certain babies have a problem with the part of the brain that controls breathing and how they wake.

Whatever the true reasons, cot death can occur not just overnight in the cot, but also during a nap at any time of day. For reasons that are not fully understood, it also seems to be more common during winter. The second month is when most deaths occur and nearly 90% of cot deaths happen in babies under six months, with the risk reducing as the baby grows older. Very few cot deaths take place after one year old.

Among the statistical data some interesting trends appear. Where recorded, the cot death rate for babies with fathers in routine and manual occupations was more than twice that with fathers in the managerial and professional group. And, again for reasons that aren't known, SIDS also seems relatively uncommon in Asian families.

So there's a lot we don't know, but what do we know about the risk factors and how to mitigate against them? While there's no way to guarantee the prevention of cot death there are a widely accepted set of steps which can help keep your baby safe.

> ➤ Cut out smoking in pregnancy, that's both of you – and once your baby is born don't let anyone smoke in the same room as your baby. It really is worth turning into an anti-smoking nazi once you become a dad.

> ➤ Place your baby on her back to sleep – and not on the front or side.

> Do not let your baby get too hot, and keep her head uncovered while she sleeps and/or while she is indoors in general.

> Place your baby with her feet to the foot of the cot, to prevent her wriggling down under the covers. You can use a baby sleep bag from three months onwards.

> Never sleep with your baby on a sofa or armchair. By far the safest place for your baby to sleep is in a crib or cot in a room with you for the first six months.

> It's particularly dangerous for your baby to sleep in your bed if you or your partner:

>> are a smoker, even if you never smoke in bed or at home
>> have been drinking alcohol
>> take medication or drugs that make you feel drowsy
>> are just very tired (which you will be), or
>> if your baby was born before 37 weeks or weighed less than 2.5kg or 5½ lbs at birth.

> Using a dummy to settle your baby to sleep can reduce the risk of cot death according to some studies, potentially because the handle of the dummy keeps air flow open if they end up on their front. The advice is if you plan to breastfeed make sure you are well established before introducing the dummy.

> Breastfeeding itself is also thought to reduce the risk.

In other areas, the debate around SIDS is an ongoing and, in some cases, a confusing one. For example, how useful are baby movement monitors that sound an alarm if they cannot detect a baby's breathing movement?

Another contentious issue is around swaddling. This ancient technique of pacifying infants has made something of a comeback in recent years.

But recent research has advised parents to proceed with caution – a view echoed by the leading body in the field, the Foundation for the Study of Infant Death.

What is key to remember is that cot death is uncommon and becomes increasingly rare after the age of five months – which is about the time when babies are able to roll over and move a bit under their own steam. The measures listed above reduce the small risk of cot death even further. If you can, try not to let this nasty unsolved mystery play on your mind constantly to the point that it becomes debilitating for you, your partner and ultimately your baby.

Words from your fellow fathers

Murray, father of two: *Lack of sleep was the worst bit of the whole thing and the major factor in nearly every argument we had. I think we both suffered really badly.*

Nick, father of two: *I found the lack of sleep the toughest, it is not the first night of no sleep – to be honest we have all been through no sleep in our lives pre-babies – you just deal with it. The thing that is hard is the constant lack of sleep, you can never catch up. It goes on and on day after day. You have to change your lifestyle in the first few months (I didn't). It is not the all night of not sleeping either, it is being woken in the night (even if you aren't doing anything) and the early morning and late nights due to feeding the baby. It is the broken sleep, that lack of quality sleep.*

Winston, father of two: *Even four years into being a dad, I never sleep for eight hours solid. I may well have had my last night of unbroken sleep. I didn't used to look my age but I do now.*

Ben, father of two: *The adrenalin is incredible when you have a baby and I think we both managed well for the first couple of* *months but it hit us both around three months when you are just worn down by it all.*

You just have to take it in turns to get a lie in, afternoon doze, anything. Never ever turn down the opportunity of sleep, even if it is just at traffic lights, preferably when they are on red.

The first time for absolutely everything

Having your first child changes your entire life, everybody knows that.

On all sorts of serious, grown-up levels becoming a dad can rearrange the furniture in your head and give your emotions a good rinsing at the same time.

But as well as the profound stuff, fatherhood also does something much more prosaic. It takes the confident, worldly, knowing man that you no doubt are and busts you back to the status of a novice.

Within these first three months you and your partner will face a bewildering barrage of situations for which you can call on very few frames of reference.

Whether it's seeing your baby smile for the first time (and wanting to strangle the fifth person to tell you that it's just wind) or changing a nappy that looks like a war has been fought in it, it's safe to say that this is a period in your life when new things will happen to you on an almost daily basis.

The first big cry

Chances are your baby will have cried in hospital, she may have even cried the moment her little head hit the air. But there is often a moment once you've got home when for the very first time you and your partner are witness to your immediate future.

'Wow, she's got a great set of lungs on her' you'll say nervously. Inwardly you'll be thinking 'I can't take that, that's not a cry, it's an artillery onslaught, a non-stop barrage of noise sharper and more penetrating than any bullet.'

'Hasn't she just?', your partner will say, inwardly smiling as you get to hear what she had to deal with on her own in hospital for the past few nights.

Crying is designed solely to grab your attention and evolution has engineered it so the noise is as effective as possible at doing just that. In fact it is so powerful that some women can lactate just by hearing a cry and it doesn't even have to emanate from *their* baby.

So don't worry if crying gets to you, it's meant to.

Your part of the bargain as parent and protector is to try and work out what has caused the cry and remedy it. The term 'easier said than done' could well have been coined in response to this very situation.

The perceived wisdom is that they are either hungry, tired, lonely or uncomfortable – the latter covering anything from a dirty nappy to wind and temperature.

In recent years the 'science' of interpreting what each type of cry means has moved from the realms of mother's intuition to big business. There are even iPhone apps that purport to tell you what your baby wants.

The Dunstan Baby Language system,[6] for instance, claims to have isolated each cry to a remarkable degree and lists the different sounds as:

- Neh   I'm hungry
- Owh   I'm sleepy
- Heh   I'm experiencing discomfort
- Eh   I have wind
- Eairh   I have lower wind
- Ey Wassup I've been allowed to watch too much telly.

While I may well have misremembered the final one they are big claims, although not ones that have been scientifically verified in any significant way.

Even if you can speak fluent baby, you'll still no doubt find yourself in a situation where sating your relentlessly crying child is seemingly impossible. The stress this can cause, especially when you throw in chronic fatigue, is not to be underestimated. Working as a team to help each other out is crucial but if you are on your own, take deep breaths, remember that your baby is doing all it knows how to do and that it will pass.

Honestly.

The first nasty nappy change

Whoever does the PR for nappy changing needs a talking to, it's not that bad.

All right, on occasions you'll put your finger in something disagreeable, but at least it's your baby's disagreeable produce. If, by some freak of nature, you are unlucky enough to find yourself changing the nappy of someone else's child you will come to see your own offspring's excrement in a whole new and favourable light.

Technique-wise, disposable nappies are as straightforward as it gets and gone are the days when you needed advanced origami to pin a towelling nappy together. (If you are planning to go with the old-style nappies by the way, I doff my cap to you and also say a little prayer.)

A few little tips are worth knowing. First there are the three Ps – Preparation Prevents Pootastrophy. A fully stocked changing table is a beautiful thing. Once you open the Pandora's Box of a full nappy, putting a lid back on it again while you try and find some baby wipes is not an easy thing to do.

Likewise if you are doing a change on the hoof, have the essential kit within arm's length or woe betide both you and that nice clean t-shirt you've got on.

When you do open things up, try and use the inside front part of the nappy to get the first wipe in. It will collect a very decent amount of poo from the soft little bottom of your cherub and will leave you just the detritus to deal with. Graphic, I know, but you'll be thankful of it.

As babies get a bit older, they often don't like having their nappy changed and distraction is the key here. The fear of your little one getting her hands in her own doings as you clean up, lives with all of us at every nappy change. If it happens, you are in the lap of the gods, as what is essentially a dirty protest unfolds before your very eyes. Perhaps the best thing to do is just revel in your baby's creativity as she cave paints all over your white wall or – especially if you have a boy – creates a charming water feature right there in your living room.

You're not truly a dad until you have a face full of something nasty.

The first smile

Your baby's first proper social smile can occur as early as four weeks post-birth – and after the month or so you and your partner will likely have had, a little bit of a reward will be gratefully received.

As ever, the timings of this joyous happening can vary a lot, so don't worry that you have spawned a mini Morrissey if you don't get belly laughs when you're expecting them.

If you are lucky enough to see a smile even earlier than the four-week mark, don't let any sour-faced fool dismiss it as wind – smile right back and let the love in.

As well as being a beautiful thing to witness, early smiles play a big part in your baby's seemingly innate desire to communicate with the two most important people in its life. From very early on they can imitate the facial gestures of their parents – try sticking your tongue out, even to a newborn.

Your little one is programmed to hold your gaze and engage you in a social tête à tête – which has you hooked right from the off.

The time you spend gazing into your baby's eyes won't just lower your stress levels, but will be a key part of the development of your baby and the bond you share with her.

So say cheese.

The first bath

Nervy one this, and definitely a team sport – the four hands that you and your partner can muster hardly seem enough in the early days.

Getting the temperature right is crucial and not that easy first up. So petrified was I of putting our beautiful baby into scalding hot water that I had the tendency to put him in what was essentially an ice bath instead. An experience he did not enjoy.

Spending a few quid on a little plastic thermometer which tells you when it is spot on is a good move, if you don't trust the age-old trick of testing the temperature with your elbow.

Even when the water is perfect, the first few bathtimes can still be a little unsettling for all concerned. Strangely enough new-born babies don't always react well to either being naked and exposed, or being lowered back first into a strange wet bowl.

So with a hand to support the neck and head and the other one under the body the trick is to slide the baby as gently as gently can be into the water, feet first. Once she is in, you become acutely aware that you are essentially holding a live salmon in your hands. Coupled with the frighteningly painful position you have put your back into as you leant over the bath, you begin to wonder if you will ever move again.

Once you do bring the event to a close, you'll immediately be grateful that your partner remembered to lay out the 23 individual items you will now instantly need to keep your baby warm and very quickly get them dry and dressed.

A palaver, yes, but fast forward a month or two and bathtimes will be a doddle, such a well-seasoned dunker will you have become.

The first cold

Babies are full of snot.

For what seems like months, they snort and snuffle their way through the night and make you sit bolt upright time after time as they seemingly struggle to breathe.

Then they get a cold.

What you thought was bad, was in fact nasal normality and now they have the snuffles plus an infection and it knocks them for six. You watch helplessly as their tiny nose streams, their little pigeon chest heaves and they even go off their beloved milk.

Because her immune system is still developing, the chances are your baby will probably get about eight colds in her first year alone. This amounts to an awful lot of disturbed nights for everyone. But strangely enough, she probably won't get a cold until after three months, as up until then, she is protected by maternal antibodies that are still in her system from pregnancy.

Given that a nipper's cold can hang around for up to two weeks before it gets fought off, you'll soon begin to wonder if anything other than mucus actually exists in the world, as one infection rolls inexorably into the next. A big problem lies in the fact that babies can't actually breathe through their mouths, but only through their noses for the first five months or so.

And what can you do to help? Not much, unfortunately. When they get past three months you too will worship at the altar of infant painkillers which can bring down fever and make them generally feel less shit. Keeping them hydrated is important, too, so if they struggle to feed for the normal length of time because of breathing issues, offer it to them as little and often if possible.

Actually shifting the mucus is tricky. Saline drops squirted up the nose work well, and are used regularly in hospitals, but to say babies hate having them applied would be a substantial understatement. There are also aspirators on the market which claim to be able to remove the excess snot by the power of suction – essentially reverse bogie bellows. Almost everyone seems to buy one, but few have the heart to use them.

Plug in vaporisers, liquid capsules and chest rubs all come in to play past three months, but for now the biggest thing you've got to offer your little one as they struggle through is love and cuddles.

If at any point you are even mildly worried go and see your GP. Not wanting to trouble anyone isn't an option when they are this small, especially if it's your first and you've not got anything to compare it to.

The first travel cot battle

Just to get this straight, every time is like the first time you put a travel cot up.

When it works well, life is good, when it goes off on one of its illogical and infuriating wanderings, the Marx Brothers in their pomp couldn't have choreographed a more farcical scene.

This side stays up, that one doesn't. That one stays up, this one doesn't.

After much push-me-pull-you nonsense and with your baby's bedtime approaching at a frightening speed you gird your loins, pull up the middle and launch a surprise attack on the insurgent outer arms.

Nothing.

The situation is critical and you are sweating and swearing in a way not befitting either a new father or a guest in someone else's home.

Reinforcements are needed – don't worry who, anyone in the house will do. The moment your ally approaches, your travel cot enemy will sense that humiliation is almost complete and will become putty in their hands, gently complying with their every movement.

Swines.

Words from your fellow fathers

Tom, father of two: *I think the hardest thing early on is working out what to do when they make noises you can't possibly identify – it's like looking under the car bonnet, realising you need a mechanic, then it dawning on you that you have to take responsibility to sort it yourself.*

Marcus, father of four: *The travel cot was the most challenging piece of equipment. In truth I've never managed it and it's still my wife's job.*

Suki, father of three: *The biggest shock was probably that first explosive nappy and the thought that the only way to deal with the situation was to plonk the baby into the bath.*

These are the times you have to stay calm and rely on a plentiful supply of wet wipes.

Rob, father of two: *I remember throwing the travel cot across the room at one point because it was so difficult to put up.*

The baby wasn't in it at the time, of course.

Looking after the grown-ups

Shall I be Mother?

It's hard to imagine another area of life when something so fundamentally and earth-shatteringly draining as delivering a baby would be followed immediately by another happening that in many ways is even more taxing.

But that's what your partner is facing as she arrives home from hospital. Regardless of whether the birth went without a hitch or a stitch, under any other circumstances it would be bed rest, book reading and back rubs all round for the recovering patient.

That kind of recuperation is a very hard trick to pull off when there's a newborn politely letting you know in their own inimitable way that they are feeling hungry or have an air bubble trapped inside them that feels the size of a Ford Galaxy.

Which is where you come in.

Physical recovery

There's no nice way of saying this, but new mothers bleed a lot after they have given birth.

It's not the sort of thing that mums say to mums-to-be, it's not even the sort of thing fathers of a different generation may have been aware of – but it happens and you should be ready for it.

No matter if she's had a vaginal or caesarean birth, this bleeding, called lochia, is how the body gets rid of the lining of the womb after birth.

The blood may come out in gushes and include clots or flow more evenly like a heavy period. More often than not, it will change colour from the initial bright red and become lighter as the uterus heals and returns to its normal size.

Your partner may bleed for as little as two to three weeks or as long as six weeks after having the baby. Generally, other than taking it easy, keeping an eye on the colour and amount of the flow and stocking up on maternity pads (tampons are a no-no, as they can cause infection) it's just a case of waiting for it to finish.

It's far from plain sailing, though. You should call the midwife or doctor immediately if your partner:

> has a tender tummy

> has a fever or a chill

> passes clots bigger than a 50p piece

> has bleeding that stays heavy and red for more than the first week

> has bleeding with an unpleasant smell.

Occasionally, bleeding that's much heavier than normal can occur between 24 hours and six weeks after birth. It is called secondary postpartum haemorrhage and it's thought that fewer than one new mum in 100 experiences it.

Your partner could also have a wound between her vagina and back passage, an area called the perineum. She will need to keep this part of her body clean to prevent infection there too, and although they sound painful, salt baths can do a world of good and can actually be soothing.

While bleeding is a very common and widespread postnatal issue, there are a whole host of others that can make an appearance too, just when your partner could do without it, such as constipation, skin problems and incontinence.

She's been in the wars in a big way and a big part of your new dad duties are to be there to make like as easy and pain free as possible for her as she gets to grips with the gargantuan job of being a mother. If she is recovering from a caesarean delivery, you are going to be a very busy boy indeed.

C-section births

Even though it is quite obvious that a caesarean is major surgery in every sense of the word, the after-effects and the pain it causes can still take a newly babied couple by surprise.

It can hurt to cough, to laugh, to shuffle around in bed, to do almost anything in fact. Thank goodness your partner can recover properly with lots of stress-free rest and blissful peace and quiet.

Ah.

Just because your partner didn't have a vaginal birth, it doesn't mean she won't have heavy vaginal bleeding after the birth. If it was an emergency C-section there's a good chance ventouse or forceps were given a go too, which may mean further stitches in the perineum.

It's tough and it's down to you to help make it better by taking some of the strain of new motherhood on your broad shoulders, even if they are hunched through fatigue.

First things first, your partner needs to eat and drink well and keep her wound clean and safe. Despite what her body may be telling her, she needs to get up and take the first ginger steps toward mobility as often as she feels able.

Breastfeeding is a hard enough skill to crack without being wracked with pain every time you move. The good news is that once they start, women are just as likely to breastfeed their baby successfully after a C-section as they are after having had a vaginal birth. Helping her to get comfortable before she starts a feed is your job. It's a vital one, given that the first few days and weeks of breastfeeding are critical to establishing a pattern and environment that will work for both mother and baby.

Lifting of any sort is out, including lifting older children. Any jobs that involve stretching are also off limits as is being too proud to accept help. If friends or family offer, accept it. If they don't, offer for them.

Keeping visitors down to a minimum for this first week or two – except for those who will pull their weight and come armed with a shepherd's pie so large it could have its own postcode – is another very smart thing for you to take control of. As much as you want to show off what is undoubtedly the most beautiful baby ever born, it will be even more beautiful the following week so try and resist the temptation to have a totally open house – your partner, despite in some cases what she might be saying, really does need to rest and get to know the new person in her life.

As the days and weeks go by, things get easier and as far as driving is concerned, despite reports to the contrary, very few motor insurance policies stipulate the need for post C-section women to take a set amount of time off the road. It's down to how she feels she would cope with the likes of an emergency stop and the view of her doctor or midwife.

Your partner may be up and at 'em within a few days of being home, but for many women the post-caesarean spell is a difficult time when they rely heavily on their partners and other kith and kin to help them through.

The emotional recovery

After such a crescendo of emotions and hormonal upheaval suffered by your partner, it's inevitable that there will be, for want of a better phrase, a come-down after the birth.

The 'baby blues' is the name given to that process and the often weepy and irritable mood which it brings about. It's estimated that something like 80% of new mothers experience this crash back down to earth. It's thought to be linked to hormonal adjustments the body makes two to four days after the baby is born.

Add in an often daunting new sense of responsibility, post-birth pain, tear of failure and a nice dollop of dog-tiredness and you've got the potential to feel tremendously overwhelmed.

Your first role is as bouncer to keep visitor numbers down. But perhaps the most vital thing for you to do through this spell is listen and be there for her to cry on or rage at if she needs to. In most cases, the baby blues pass as quick as they arrived and are a necessary, if intense, part of the healing process.

If things persist though, or baby blues symptoms reoccur much past a month after having the baby, something more serious could be afoot.

Postnatal depression

It wasn't too long ago that postnatal depression (PND) was seen as a rarity among mothers.

The figure that was bandied around of one in 10 mums suffering has since been revised to more like one in four.

As the stigma around mental illness is slowly dismantled piece by piece, more mothers are recognising the symptoms and, crucially, seeking help. Rather than seeing the statistical change as proof of an epidemic, perhaps we should give thanks that at least now far fewer women are suffering in silence.

As with all mental health issues, spotting the relevant symptoms either in oneself or in someone you are close to can be a fiendishly complex area. To add to the difficulty, the existence of the baby blues muddies the waters slightly, but the medical advice is clear when it comes to distinguishing between the two. While the baby blues are short-lived and often disappear without treatment, the opposite is true of PND.

Tell-tale signs and symptoms are different for every mother, which is why your role and that of your close family and friends is crucial in identifying behaviour or feelings that are unusual for the person you know so well.

Broadly speaking, a real sense of hopelessness, anxiety, guilt or loneliness can all be key signs. Exhaustion and a feeling of being trapped are also symptomatic and given the lack of sleep and huge life change new mothers go through these can often be put down to something other than genuine mental distress. But if you sense your partner is overwhelmed by any of these feelings and that the black cloud just isn't shifting, it could well be PND.

The illness often creeps up on mothers around four to six weeks after the birth of the baby, but it can and does come out of nowhere months afterwards, too.

The reasons why PND strikes and why some people are more vulnerable to it than others are largely unknown. Brain chemistry, genetics, reaction to hormonal changes, diet – they've all been postulated and researched but as yet no real answers have been found. What's for sure is that isolation when coping with a new baby, being away from family and friends, can be an enormous factor, as can the strain an awful lot of women find trying to breastfeed.

If you are worried that your partner is suffering from PND, you need to come to the party in a big way.

First, gently encouraging her to speak to a health visitor or GP about how she is feeling is crucial. If she's nervous or scared, offer to go with her if it helps – and keep reassuring about just how common and beatable PND is.

You'll also need to take a lot of the strain off her and may well need some time away from work to make that possible. Take care you don't charge in and take over, that will only make her feel worse. Offer to take on jobs and help her to prioritise what she is taking on.

Exercise is increasingly seen as a key tool in beating depression, so make time for her go to the gym, walk or swim or whatever she fancies. If she's not been finding the time to eat well, you can help to put that right too.

But perhaps the most important thing of all is that you listen to her and reassure her that she's a great mum, and that you love her very much.

Be under no illusion, though, supporting someone with PND is tough and you'll need to take care of yourself, too. Organisations such as the Association for Postnatal Illness (http://apni.org) can help you help your partner through what can be a frightening and bewildering time.

Once a diagnosis has been made, there are a lot of treatment options on offer and with the right help it is a very beatable illness, despite how your partner may feel while she is in its grip.

Most GPs can refer sufferers to support groups, counsellors or psychotherapists. Cognitive behavioural therapy (CBT), which teaches everyday coping strategies, is becoming a popular route.

Antidepressants are the other option. These work by raising the levels of the hormone serotonin. Between five and seven out of every 10 women who take antidepressants report that their symptoms lessen within a few weeks of taking them.

However, these drugs have been shown to pass into breastmilk, although in very small amounts – so it's far from an easy choice. Speaking to your GP to get a clear assessment of the risks and benefits involved is vital.

As is, if recent studies are anything to go by, your own mental health; because it seems that men get postnatal depression too.

Men and postnatal depression

There's a growing body of thought that suggests that many new fathers have been experiencing PND, with scores of cases going undetected. A US study[7] put the number of cases at around one in 10 (the same number that female PND was thought to be prevalent at for many years).

Life changes, new responsibilities, lack of sleep or supporting a wife with postnatal depression were cited as the potential triggers by the Eastern Virginia Medical School academics. The research also found that new fathers tended to be happiest in the first few weeks after the baby was born, with depression taking hold after three to six months.

These are extreme cases, but don't underestimate the potential impact having a baby will have on you mentally. Being the breadwinner and little else isn't an option for, or often a desire of, many men today. We want to be involved and engaged, to play a big part in bringing up our children as well as providing for them.

And it can take its toll.

Men and women tend to react differently to stress and it's said that men with depression get mad, while women get sad.

While this is a generalisation, an increase in alcohol consumption, self-medicating or even having affairs can all be signs of mental anxiety and disquiet in men. Becoming a father is a big deal and it's all too easy for men to ignore their own health when pride and the stiff upper lip kicks in.

Just as air safety announcements tell us to apply our own mask before helping others, taking the time to look after yourself isn't a selfish act, it's the exact opposite.

Words from your fellow fathers

Ben, father of two: *Once your wife has a baby I don't think any rational man can look at the fairer sex again without thinking 'Hats off to you'.*

If men had children, caesarean sections would have been invented before the wheel.

Rob, father of two: *The recovery period was very tough because my wife had an operation to deliver the baby.*

I helped her with feeds, changing nappies and waking in the night to attend to the baby. I also cooked throughout that period – so I think I was brilliant!

Jason, father of two: *Second time around was a C-section so six weeks of taking it easy means Dad has his hands full.*

Initially we did consider getting her a bell to ring for my service. I really enjoyed looking after her and the boys, though.

Marcus, father of four: *Looking back I think my wife did suffer from postnatal depression, although I doubt she would admit it today.*

Winston, father of two: *I wasn't depressed, I think I might have mourned my previous, happy-go-lucky life but I wasn't depressed. Fortunately, I was a happy dad in a stable relationship and always felt lucky.*

Colin, father of two: *I don't think I suffered from depression, but can quite believe dads can get it.*

Such highs and lows of emotions – stress, elation, pressure, fear, pride, guilt – are all experienced in a very short space of time with very little sleep, so it must affect some people that way.

Simon, father of one: *Male postnatal depression? Sounds like bollocks to me.*

Your progress report

Your baby

As we've seen, your baby is making remarkable progress before your very eyes on a daily basis during the first three months – with brain development leading the way.

Over this period your little one will change from a watery-eyed, floppy-limbed *Alien*-like creature to being capable of holding her head up, tracking objects with her eyes and even smiling at you.

Never again will she learn so much so fast – she'll even begin to recognise you and your partner from the seven billion other people on the planet – clever.

Sleeping could also start to take a semblance, by which I mean not very much 'blance' at all, of regularity and order, and you'll also start to see a schedule of sorts around eating and pooing.

What I'm trying to say is that your tiny little tot, all innocent and sweet, will throughout these three months, begin to enforce their routine on you, your home and your entire life. Muhahhhhhha.

Your partner

We've seen in detail what a tough time this can be for your partner, from recovering after the birth to the trials of breastfeeding and the spectre of postnatal depression.

But let's not get too carried away with the black paintbrush, shall we? Many new mothers, while it's undoubtedly a tough sleep-deprived time, are also experiencing the most intense and emotionally powerful period of their lives as they bond in quite spectacular fashion with their child.

This bonding process can be amazing to watch and be around, although some dads do report feeling a touch left out as a love affair unfolds in front of them – which leads us on to. . .

You

If you do feel your nose being put slightly out of joint by the closeness of the bond between mother and child know this; your time will come.

In this initial spell it's easy to feel a bit of a spare part where the baby is concerned. Remember that every cuddle you give and every gaze you hold is working to cement you as one of the two most important people in this little person's life.

If you possibly can just revel in the moment, embrace every 3am wake up, relish every nuzzle, soak it up and file it away. The first three months are rock hard for sure, but they are also magical, unique and fleeting.

MONTHS 4-6

Getting down to business

Y ou've been a dad for more than 12 weeks now – that's over 80 consecutive days of fatherhood under your belt.

You are a master.

Kind of.

After a while the visitors stop coming, the shepherd's pies cease to materialise and you and your partner are often left relatively well alone to enjoy your baby.

While everyone's experiences will be different, there are three key things that, more likely than not, will be true about your life during the next three months.

You'll be back at work and the 'but I've just had a baby' line will be wearing pretty thin as an excuse for your tardiness and all-round poor showing.

Your baby will almost certainly be waking up at least once a night.

Your tiny new arrival will have generated more jobs to do in your home than you ever dreamed possible.

This tricky triumvirate combines to create what politicians call a 'challenging environment', when what they actually mean is a living nightmare.

I'm painting an overly dark picture, but there is no denying that you will become very interested indeed in the answer to a few fundamental questions. How can you get your little angel to sleep in a way which allows you to feel like card-carrying members of the human race, if not actually looking like them?

How can we do what needs to be done at home without tearing each other limb from limb in indignant rage as we lay side by side in bed thinking *'Surely they can't think it's MY turn!?'*

And how can we both weave the very occasional conversation with friends, fellow parents and even, heaven forbid, people without children into our chaotic lives to help keep us sane?

Tricky questions one and all. Let's go for the big one first, sleep.

The S word: Part 2

Once your baby has adjusted to being on planet Earth over the course of its first few months, you stand a chance of establishing a semblance of a sleep routine back into your domestic world.

As you've probably noticed, on average a three-month-old baby will sleep twice as much as their parents, but half of this will be in the daytime. On average your baby will sleep for blocks of about two hours in the day, and four to six hours at night.

Just like us grown-ups, babies fluctuate between deep and light sleep all night; in fact from six months onwards your baby was establishing sleep patterns while they were still in the womb.

Babies do some serious dreaming too, spending almost half of their kip time in the REM state that leads to it. With dreamtime seen as vital for filing away and making sense of our experiences, you can see why a baby, for whom almost every waking second represents a discovery of mindblowing magnitude, would need more than its fair share of the stuff.

As your little one grows she will gradually sleep more during the night and less in the day. At this stage, on average, she will be sleeping twice as long at night as in the day – or so the story goes.

These daytime naps gradually coalesce to become a bit longer and less frequent by the six-month mark. By the time they reach 12 months, most babies will have one or two daytime naps before eventually these sleeps are dropped as they move through toddlerdom and only sleep at night.

Way before that milestone is reached, though, balancing the daytime naps against the night time sleep is the game you'll be playing. Obvious as it sounds, the more your baby sleeps during the day the less she will sleep at night – worth considering as you luxuriate during that three-hour lunchtime nap – you may pay later! But don't go too far the other way: babies need sleep in the day; otherwise they will get *too* tired and then not sleep well anyway. It's a fine line.

Another tricky area revolves around the classic vision of parents dismantling the doorbell, manoeuvring round the squeaky floorboard and tiptoeing up the stairs to ensure junior isn't disturbed one iota. When you consider that all babies have essentially been listening to the sounds of your home through the thin wall of the womb for at least a couple of months before they arrived, you begin to realise that a relatively normal noise level is the way to go.

This is borne out by just how quickly an awful lot of babies are soothed or even drop off when they hear the sound of the extractor fan in the kitchen or the vacuum cleaner in the lounge. So potent are these white noises that you can purchase entire albums of household implement racket on iTunes so you can use them to induce sleep wherever you are, without turning your baby's nursery into a Curry's showroom.

Despite this novel little trick, your baby's need for constant feeding, her propensity to be disturbed by wind in a quite extraordinary way and the fact that her sleep patterns will mean she enters light sleep up to five times a night, all mean that a decent night's sleep will be a rarity at best and a fleeting memory at worst.

An often controversial little device that parents have turned to for many a long year can help.

To do the dummy?

Few things are as divisive in the world of parenting as the dummy. Some swear by them, some loathe them, some do both and are driven to use them behind closed doors, keeping them from public view like a dirty little secret.

What's for sure is that they have been around for donkey's years and they work as a way of getting your baby to ease themselves into the land of nod as they soothe themselves via the action of sucking.

As well as the obvious advantages of dummy use, there's some evidence that they can help to prevent cot death by preventing the airway being blocked. However, putting your baby on her back and not smoking anywhere near her remain by far and away the most important prevention methods.

On the negative side, prolonged use of a dummy is said to increase the risk of ear, chest and stomach infections. Also, the longer your baby uses a dummy, especially if they are still using it past the age of three, the more likely it is to cause changes in the way their teeth grow – which can result in an over or crossbite.

Using a dummy could also affect your baby's speech development a little further down the line for the simple reason that they have their mouth full a lot of the time. The recommendation is that you use a dummy only for settling your baby to sleep and not during the day.

All in all, dummies, when used sparingly, are a viable and sometimes much-needed option that can give you and your partner a well-earned break as well as helping to calm a distressed baby. However, do weigh up the pros and cons before embarking on the dummy, and if you can cope without it, parents and health professionals alike will applaud you.

As with breast vs bottle, once you've made your decision, try to avoid beating yourself to a pulp about it. In life's rich tapestry it is but a trifling thing really. If you do decide to go down the dummy route, try and use an orthodontic or flat dummy which can help the mouth develop more naturally than the traditional rounded ones.

Keep the dummy as clean and sterile as possible, change it regularly and don't dip it in sugar or whisky no matter what any older relatives may suggest.

For many, getting rid of the dummy happens naturally before the first birthday is reached as the baby begins to spit it out and get themselves back to sleep without it.

But some youngsters can grow to love their dummy for a long time and the longer you wait to get shot of it the more of a palaver and emotional tug of war it can become – but we will deal with that further down the line.

Aside from the soother, is there anything else you can do to make your baby more content, sleep better and develop a routine that fits hand in glove with your idea of a perfect day and night?

You had to go and ask didn't you?

The Baby Wars

Having a strategy to help you cope with bringing up a baby is nothing new. The long bracing walk in the perambulator, the journey in the car or the lullaby – have all been popular and passed on down the years.

What has changed is the proliferation of working mums, their time stretched to the limit and also the ability of tens of thousands of people to gather together online and essentially beat the virtual meconium out of each other over what the best way to bring up baby really is.

The chances are your partner's bedside table will be heaving under the weight of a goodly number of books, all of which outline a different route to baby happiness. There's one approach in particular that has caused more debate than all the rest combined, Gina Ford's *The Contented Little Baby Book* (Vermilion).

First published in 1999, it has sold by the carry cot load and has established its author as the undisputed queen of routine. Ford advises new parents to break down their day into five-minute slots with the baby being woken and fed by 7am. Subsequent feeds and naps are slotted in at set times up until the final feed of the day, during which parents should not make eye contact with their baby in case it gets excited before bedtime.

The end game of all of this is to deliver not just a contented baby, but one who sleeps through the night like a dream.

To say that this method produce Marmite reactions in parents would be doing this book's impact a severe disservice. For those who love her methods Ford is a heroine, a woman who has singlehandedly given them back their lives and their sanity, restored order and calm to their household and allowed them to retain at least a semblance of their former lives.

For working mums in particular it has been a boon, it seems, meaning the sleep they need to juggle their two jobs is on tap and their baby can be minded by someone else with ease as long as they watch the clock and follow the plan.

For those who disagree with her approach Ford has been labelled Public Enemy Number One. Such is the venom with which some of her detractors have a swipe at Ford's techniques, she took legal action against the website Mumsnet in 2006 and in 2010 even the Deputy Prime Minister Nick Clegg had a pop, calling her approach 'absolute nonsense'.

Out of the smoky battlefield there does seem to be a middle way emerging, though. There's little doubt that babies seem happier when their day follows some sort of semi regular pattern – your first overnight stay in a strange house will probably demonstrate that to you pretty well. Whether or not that routine needs to be drilled to the nearest five minutes is a moot point. While the online battle still rages about the Fordian approach, there are also plenty of people prepared to admit they subscribe to the routine approach, but not necessarily with as much military vim and vigour as is suggested by some.

One area that seems to have gathered controversial steam rather than shed it, is the notion of letting the baby 'cry it out' as they attempt to drop off or wake during a sleep.

Controlled crying

As you or your partner haul your sorry backsides out of bed for the fourth time in as many hours to rock your baby to sleep, life can seem really quite bleak.

Will this ever end? Will I make it through a day at work without curling up in the corner of a crowded lift and drifting into blissful rest? Will we ever find a way to crack the sleep problem?

Or perhaps getting up is long gone, perhaps you find yourself ousted from your own bed, your baby having moved in on a semi-permanent basis, feeding on demand from dusk till dawn.

Whatever your scenario, if you and your partner are consistently denied the kip you need, there's a very good chance you will have the 'controlled crying' conversation. While there are many controlled crying methods, the general gist is that you leave your baby to cry for slightly increasing spells which are punctuated by you entering the room and either physically comforting them or just verbally reassuring them before leaving again.

When it works, parents can find that after just a handful of admittedly often horrendous days they have a baby who settles herself to sleep and stays asleep – or at least drops back off on her own when and if she wakes.

But at what cost?

Research suggesting long-term behavioural damage can be caused by the crying baby's brain being flooded with the stress hormone cortisol can be found side-by-side with other studies which suggest nothing of the sort takes place.[8] Not particularly helpful at 3.47am when you have discussed the merits of letting her cry for the third time that night.

There are no clear-cut answers I'm afraid, but what is for certain is that listening to your baby cry out and resisting the urge to go to them is one of the toughest things you'll ever attempt.

If you find yourself with a baby who has become thoroughly used to being rocked to sleep and screams like a banshee at the merest hint of a cot sheet coming into contact with their soft little cheek, one alternative to controlled crying is the pick up/put down method.

Initially championed by the late Tracey Hogg in her popular *Baby Whisperer* books, it involves picking the crying baby up, comforting her until she is calm and then putting her down again.

Then repeat ad infinitum until baby gets herself to sleep.

Hogg reckons this procedure takes 20 minutes on average, although admits it can run over the hour mark, by which time not only will your baby be asleep, you will have pecs like a super steroidal bodybuilder.

However, health professionals now only advocate controlled crying for babies over four months old, and recommend that you do not pick your baby up, but comfort her in her cot.

Whatever way you choose to try and crack the sleep problem – and there are no quick fixes – the most important thing is that you and your partner both support each other and try, try like the wind, to retain even a semblance of a sense of humour as you battle through. Not easy I know, but laughing hysterically in the wee small hours is a much better option than adding to your wretchedness by having an argument as the sun comes up on another busy day.

Talking of which, have you noticed that there's rather a lot to do now you have a baby in the house?

Words from your fellow fathers

Steve, father of two: *We got ourselves into quite a bizarre routine with our eldest. We would stroke her forehead until she fell asleep, sometimes in the room for an hour or so, then creep out of the room on our hands and knees backwards.*

This was fine apart from we had ONE squeaky floorboard that we would always crawl onto. We'd scrunch our face up and pray this wouldn't wake her up, but it always did.

'RIGHT' I snapped one night, we are doing this controlled crying thing.

My wife couldn't cope with this and went downstairs so she couldn't hear Olivia cry (and also turned music on VERY loud to drown out the noise, oblivious to the fact this rock concert in the room underneath was not aiding the sleep process).

I left Olivia and said good night. She went crazy because she wasn't getting the princess treatment of head stroking. I waited a minute outside. Went back in, acknowledged I was still there and left for two minutes. The noise out of my little girl's mouth still amazes me to this very day. She was quite clearly unhappy with my new approach to parenting.

After eight attempts, she finally fell asleep from pure exhaustion. I repeated this for the next five days. The sixth day onwards, our lives changed for the better and she was able to fall asleep without thinking she was Victoria Beckham.

Nick, father of two: *We felt that we had to give controlled crying a go. Once you get in to picking them up, you are on the back foot. And front foot is everything in this game.*

Ben, father of two: *You have got to try controlled crying at some point in my opinion, unless you are given a real sleeper how do babies know what to do?*

Try it when you are both feeling good, as it can be full-on. Don't wait until you both are frazzled and feel you have no choice. You'll be crying as much as the baby.

Simon, father of one: *In the end we opted for a bit of controlled crying. In fairness you shouldn't use our experience as any kind of guide, our son rarely sleeps through the night still.*

Yes, we could leave him crying in his cot, in the dark, on his own at 3am but as far I'm concerned that would just make us a couple of bastards.

Return of the Baby Bomb

If you have already read *Pregnancy for Men*, my first attempt at documenting man's assent on Mount Fatherhood, you may remember the concept of the Baby Bomb.

I make no apologies for returning to it – this is one of the biggest issues in modern society and you deserve to know about it.

The effects of the Baby Bomb certainly aren't confined to these three months, nor even the three years this entire book covers. You'll feel them throughout your parenting life, if you haven't already.

I've decided to bring it up here for the simple reason that it's now, once the initial excitement is dissipating, that you are probably starting to feel the first ripples wash up on your shore.

Whereas in *Pregnancy for Men* I didn't really want to scare anyone, to make them anymore trepidatious than they already were, now that you are – to borrow a line from Robert De Niro – in the circle of trust, I can be candid.

You see, your relationship with your partner changes forever when you have a child. The terms of reference, the environment, the communication, the priorities, everything alters overnight.

This change doesn't necessarily signal the end of companionship, love and togetherness – often quite the opposite in fact – but imagining that 'and baby makes three' is the beginning, middle and end of it can lead to quite a shock for a couple of big reasons.

Equality

By and large, the modern relationship has enjoyed a period of equilibrium-inducing change over the past 30 years. A hideous generalisation, I know, but on the whole, life's decisions get made as a couple much more than they used to in our parents' or grandparents' age.

The notion that as a man you could buy a car, a house, or book a holiday without so much as a conversation with your other half is beyond laughable to most of us now. Putting the housekeeping money on the kitchen table of a Friday night for the good lady to do with as she saw fit, before retiring to the local for a pint of best and a bag of pork scratchings, may as well be a prehistoric French cave painting rather than a ritual that was performed behind millions of front doors just a generation or two ago.

The earning stats back this change up too: in 1968–69 just 5% of women brought home more money than their partner; in 2010 that figure was shown to be 44% and rising fast.[9] The breadwinning woman is a new and powerful phenomenon.

Then suddenly, into this fluid, egalitarian and gender-role-blurring reality comes a newborn child and in the time it takes to pack a baby bag women often find themselves feeling like they have been unceremoniously yanked back to 1953.

Put simply, babies are to working women what dog turds are to street performance.

While we may have changed, evolved, progressed, whatever you want to call it, at lightning pace these past 40 years, a new-born baby's *raison d'être* is almost identical to what it was centuries ago.

They aren't going to adapt to our world; we initially at least have to move very much towards theirs. With the average age of mothers giving birth having steadily risen to 29.2 years, for most women, that is a lot of adjustment – especially as careers and entire ways of life are put on hold or irrevocably altered.

It's a big deal and is something to be both aware and sympathetic of. The initial shock of becoming a mum seems to be becoming more seismic for many women because of the perceived loss of equality and hard fought-for independence they have to seemingly cede, at least temporarily. Readjustment can take a good while. You have a big part to play in making it as smooth a journey as possible and ensuring it feels like a change you'll both embrace together.

Not that you'll have bundles of time on your hands to make this happen, because the second effect of the Baby Bomb is to create more work to be taken on, a lot more work.

The division of labour

Pre-children, friction about who pulls the most weight around the home may well exist, but it is as nothing compared to what it becomes when children arrive. There's lots and lots to do, and it never ends.

Within this environment it is incredibly easy to fall into a tit-for-tat war where keeping score is endemic on both sides.

'I've been up with the baby every night this week'

'You've not done bathtime since the weekend'

'It's your turn to do breakfast'

'I've been at work all week' (Never, ever say that, ever)

Then there's the issue of not *what* you do, but *how* you do it. The slightly dramatic phrase 'domestic bullying' has been coined recently to describe a situation in which some men are increasingly finding themselves, where very little they do in terms of childcare comes up to scratch.

There's a strong element of 'men are from Mars' running through this for sure – clothes on top of the linen basket are as good as clothes in the linen basket right? Wrong – but it's also been suggested that very capable, powerful and driven career women are running their homes like they do their businesses, departments or teams. If you fall below your objectives, you are not going to enjoy your next appraisal one little bit.

Before the violins drown us out completely though, there's little doubt that as men we are most of us slaves to the expedient problem-solving streak that runs through a great many of us. Mum needs a lie-in, simple – on goes a DVD for two hours, quiet toddler, sleeping mother, problem solved.

Nappy needs changing you say? Not an issue, all clean and ready to rock in the blink of an eye. OK, so I may have changed her on the sofa to save my back or a trip upstairs to the changing table and the dirty nappy may well be left on the floor for the next six hours, but no one can deny that the original problem was sorted very quickly indeed.

In a survey by US broadcaster MSNBC, respondents were asked if the chores in their households were performed by just one person or if they were shared. A nice chunky 74% of men said jobs were done as a team, but just 51% of women said the same.

Let's be honest – this disparity probably doesn't surprise either of us does it? We do have a tendency to exaggerate our efforts just a smidgen and out of the three words 'job half done', the middle one, can, on occasion, be completely invisible to an awful lot of us.

So is that it? Are we destined to argue and mither our way through the next 18 years of our lives, both feeling underappreciated, undervalued and under the cosh?

Not necessarily. Harmony and enjoyment can flourish with the help of a few changes that – while looking simple written down here – take a goodly amount of fortitude and resolve to make happen.

First, regularly remind each other what a great job you're doing of raising your youngster and validate the feelings of exhaustion, frustration and even boredom that you both may have at different times. This is a smart move for obvious reasons. Being a parent is a remarkable thing to do, but it's real life, not a commercial. Shit stuff will happen and tedious jobs will need to be done. Occasionally feeling like you'd rather be anywhere else isn't cause for shame or finger pointing, it's cause for a hug and – in my house at least – a glass (coughs *bottle*) of wine.

Second, there's an element of giving in to be done here. For you that may mean getting off your arse a bit more and chipping in. You need to come to terms with the fact that your life really *has* changed, rather than trying to fight the fact tooth and nail. For your partner it could mean acknowledging the fact that the house may never truly be as she likes it again, or that her way may not always be the only way to get things done.

Finally, finding the time amidst all the work and the upheaval to enjoy what's happening right in front of you can bring some much-needed perspective to proceedings as you argue for the third time in a week about the best way to sterilise a teat.

Missing your children growing and developing in a blur of disinfectant wipes, frozen purée trays and games of chicken where you hope your partner will be the one to blink first and get up to see to the baby is to miss the point entirely.

We've all done it – and no one more so than me, but just occasionally if you can both agree that the washing and the emails can wait and having an hour on the floor with your beautiful baby is the way to go, you'll find that things won't seem quite so tough after all.

Words from your fellow fathers

Suki, father of three: *I would be surprised if my father ever changed a nappy!*

In those days the roles of mother and father were much more clearly defined. Now, not only are fathers expected to be much more involved in bringing up their children, they also want to be more involved and part of the whole experience and to build a relationship with their children from a young age.

The maxim 'you get out what you put in' does truly apply here.

Rob, father of two: *I think gender roles were much more defined 30–40 years ago. Nowadays both partners pitch in with all responsibilities. Or is that just in my house!?*

Murray, father of two: *We had our disagreements on the way things should be done, for sure, but I felt it was such a personal experience for my wife giving birth that she should be as comfortable as possible with all the decisions that were made.*

I think looking back she would have liked more opinions from me, but luckily we both have a similar philosophy which is largely instinctive although pretty rigid routine-wise.

Name withheld!: *Somewhere in the late 70s/early 80s a generation of men stitched us all up and caved in. One minute* *we are having cigars in the pub being treated to brandies while waiting for our wives to come back from the maternity hospital to cook tea. The next we are getting up to feed children in the middle of the night before going to work and coming back to change nappies.*

Winston, father of two: *My Dad would come home too late from work to get stuck into bathtime or feeding us. He was a more remote figure than I hope I am from my children. But he was still a great dad, it perhaps took me longer to find out.*

I think it's true that mums initially scrutinise your every movement, which is fair dos considering how much bother they have been to in acquiring the child, but my wife learnt to let me get on with things, otherwise I would never have gained the experience and knowledge of how to go about things.

Simon, father of one: *I felt the pressure. My wife was always casting a critical eye over everything I did. There were many mistakes. At which point she'd just take over and tell me to get out of the way.*

The necessity of the network

In these early months you and your partner are going to be busy bees – I think that much has probably become very clear.

The chances are your partner will be at home trying to learn how to become a mother, get her head round how much her life has changed and generally trying to cope.

In this pressurised and unfamiliar environment the ability to be able to, at the very least, talk to people going through the same thing becomes not just a good idea, but vital to keeping just the right side of deranged.

For mums there are some excellent opportunities to do just that around nowadays. The traditional route is meeting up with the bods from the

National Childbirth Trust (NCT) or other antenatal group. Not only will they be fairly local, they will also be in the same boat development-wise, which is key. The mother of a child six months older will seem like a different species at this stage as their youngster crawls around and eats raisins like they are going out of fashion. What your partner needs is a group of mums who are just as obsessed in the most microscopic details of day-to-day babydom as she is. Even if your better half thought some of them were not best mate material pre-baby, post-baby anyone who looks and feels as shagged out as they do is a friend indeed.

You may have ventured out for the awkward 'dads' night' with your antenatal class in the run up to the birth. No matter how painful that may have been, rekindle it, email them all and suggest another short get-together. You will be amazed at just what a great leveler having a baby under six months is. It will matter not one jot if the other dads you meet are the most tedious arse-numbing bores this side of Belgium, you'll only be literally talking shades of shite anyway.

Another thing you'll be coming to realise is that actually getting out of the house with a baby is not a speedy affair. The feed-change-pack-change-repack-change-feed again vortex is a powerful force not yet fully understood by science. It can keep your partner and child indoors for days on end – hence the need for some form of home-based communication.

For those very twilight zone days online forums like Mumsnet (www.mumsnet.com) and Netmums (www.netmums.com) really come into their own. In next to no time these sites have created a place where hundreds of thousands of mums can congregate with, chat to, commiserate, help, encourage and amuse each other. Mumsnet in particular has copped a bit of flak for the perceived power it now wields as a lobbying force, but at heart it is an astonishing force for good, providing mums with a sense of belonging and support when they often need it most.

While men are far from banned from sites like Mumsnet there are a few equivalents beginning to pop up for dads. None of the pretenders have grabbed the opportunity at the time of writing and made themselves *the* place for fathers online. It can only be a matter of time given the change in paternity leave which will let a father take up any remaining unpaid leave if their partner goes back to work early. This could dramatically increase the number of stay-at-home dads.

With so many of us having moved from the bosom of our families for work – or because we simply can't stand the sight of them – forming a network of other parents around you is a very smart move indeed and will serve you well for years to come. In these first few months, particularly, try and encourage your partner, if she's a little reticent, to go to the local mother and baby groups, or coffee mornings. They might seem a little forced, but they exist and thrive for good reason.

If like me, you are lucky enough at some point to have some time to be – take cover for incoming jargon – the primary caregiver for your baby, you too can experience the joy that is being the only man sat awkwardly cross-legged in a circle on the wooden floor of a library, as you join in with the fourth rendition of 'Wind the Bobbin Up' that morning.

Happy days!

Your progress report

Your baby

As well as the all-consuming business of feeding and sleeping, this three-month spell sees some real spatial awareness and body control being introduced to your baby's repertoire.

She may be strong enough to roll over from her back to her front or vice versa – which will come as a shock if she does it while you happen to be looking away. She may even start to bear her weight on those lovely little legs when you hold her arms – she's a good few months away from walking – but you are watching the very first signs of her wanting to take her first steps.

As well as general chattering and babbling on the increase, you might think you even hear the odd ma-ma and da-da, too. It's a bit early for her to be necessarily connecting them with you yet, but it still sends a tingle up your spine even if you may have imagined it from the gobbledygook of sounds. A small tip – if she is saying da-da and not ma-ma, encouraging her to say the latter rather than the former is wise.

She might start to grasp toys at this stage too, and even pass them between her hands. She could also begin to give faces she hasn't seen before a funny look. Even the early onset of teething might rear its ugly head – all pretty impressive stuff for someone who just eight weeks ago was a floppy, cross-eyed little dot.

Your partner

In between feeling exhausted and drained of all vitality as she feeds and nurtures what still is a very young baby, your partner might just be thinking or dreaming about starting to exercise and getting her pre-birth body back.

Getting back in shape after a pregnancy is a notoriously difficult thing to do. Your help in creating the time for her to do some exercise will be enormously well received. Be careful how you phrase things, mind you –'Isn't it time you went to the gym?' could land you in a world of trouble.

The psychological and physical benefits of exercise are well documented and it's a great next step on the road to recovering from the shock of the birth.

Another milestone on that road could well be the return of her periods during this spell. Occasionally this can happen even if she is still breastfeeding, but more often than not her cycle will begin when she reduces feeds or stops altogether.

You

As outlined in the Baby Bomb section earlier in this chapter, approaching the six-month mark can be when relationship issues surface, especially around childcare.

Quite often men want to and are requested to take a more active role in looking after baby by their partner – which is all good. What's not so great is the sense many men soon get as they get more involved that nothing they do is right.

From the woman's point of view you can see how this comes about – they have spent every waking moment with their baby since its birth, they know its moods, they know its cries, they know everything. Handing the responsibility for that precious thing over to dad, even just for an hour, can be an extremely tense and nerve wracking thing to do. The temptation for the mother to give advice and micro-manage the father as he tends to his baby is enormous.

Coping with what in bad cases can feel like an undermining barrage of criticism can be incredibly tough. You need to learn in your own way, too and your instincts need nurturing not crushing. If you'd have stood over your partner for the first six weeks passing negative comment on her mothering skills you'd have been a very bad man indeed.

The key to working through it, rather than hitting a stalemate that helps no one, is well-thought-out communication on your part.

Trying to have the 'please trust me to do it my way' debate in the middle of an incident where you may have been pulled up by your partner never, ever works. Emotions are running too high to have a calm, rational and open discussion so if you can, curb your instinct and address it at a neutral time with her. You'll probably find a much more sympathetic audience to your plight.

What's key to remember is that at this stage of the game you are still very much in the trenches. It might feel like after six months you should be home and hosed with this baby malarkey but that's just not the case – especially when it's your first.

You'll be doing a much better job as a couple than it may seem. If you have friends with a similar-aged tot who project an image of calm and serenity, know this – behind closed doors they will be paddling just as hard as you are to stay afloat.

MONTHS 7-9

The fog begins to lift

Don't even begin to think, not even for a moment that you are somehow out of the woods, but. . .things do begin to get a little bit more recognisable, a little bit more manageable and often a lot more enjoyable during this spell.

Don't misunderstand me, you enjoy every waking moment of being a father. Of course you do, no one is suggesting otherwise, honestly. But as your baby grows and begins to take in the world around it, you might just begin to enjoy it a little bit more, that's all.

The combination of baby starting to try something other than milk as her source of energy and even beginning to move around under her own steam somehow makes more of a difference than simply having to give her food and make sure the house is safe for her to roam. They represent the first tangible signs, albeit fledgling ones, of independence.

You can even start reading to her now, too – you could have read to her from day dot, but from now there may well be visible, even audible signs that she is enjoying it and absorbing it, which she is, by the bucketful.

Then there's the outside chance if the battle against the axis of evil that is sleep deprivation and fatigue is being at least waged, that you and your partner might actually stay awake long enough to have your first non-baby-related conversation in months. You may even rekindle a little of the fairy dust in your relationship that brought the little one into being in the first place.

Unbridled joy and happiness abounds.

Until the teeth come along, that is.

Teething is a world of pain for you and your often red-cheeked, furiously irritable, endlessly drooling little soldier – and it lasts for about two-and-a-half years.

Let's not dwell on that just yet though, chin up, your baby will soon be able to eat a banana on the move.

So proud.

Weaning, crawling and teething: your busy baby

Weaning

Weaning is another of those areas, like the best way to put your baby to sleep, where the advice given to you as parents has shifted around over the years.

The official line from the Department of Health now says that while it's best to exclusively breastfeed a baby until she is six months old, from that point on a milk-only diet doesn't give her everything she needs to thrive, with iron the main thing missing.

Until relatively recently, guidelines advised introducing babies to solid food at four months. But it's now thought that waiting those extra eight weeks reduces the baby's chance of either picking up an infection from food because her digestive system is immature or becoming poorly because her immune system isn't quite up to speed yet.

It's possible you might have a baby who just isn't satisfied with milk, even lots and lots of milk. When they begin to eat the furniture turning to solids may be unavoidable – although the advice is to avoid solids under all circumstances before the fourth month. If you do have a ravenous tot on your hands and decide to make the move between four and six months, avoid foods such as dairy products, citrus fruits and juices, eggs and shellfish. Foods that contain gluten are also worth avoiding, too, as there is evidence that early exposure can cause coeliac disease.

Other than chewing their own fingers down to the elbow the signs that your baby is ready for some proper grub are the ability to hold their head up well, sit up when they are supported, and roughly doubling their birth weight. Perhaps most telling of all, she isn't just curious about what you've got on your plate but actively tries to grab at your food – the little tinker.

Puréed or very well mashed foods like mashed spud, cooked carrots, parsnips, banana, stewed apple or pear are a great way to start. As are baby cereal or rice mixes which you can stir into their milk as a gentle introduction to something a bit more substantial.

Gently does it. Be careful not to fall into the clean plate trap – the amount you make as a portion doesn't tally perfectly with the amount that will fill them up – why would it? They have tiny stomachs at this stage and offering a spoonful or two can often be enough.

There's no hard or fast rule about when to try them out on their first solids, before a milk feed, after or even during, whatever works best for your child. Don't be surprised if whatever you lovingly serve up gets spat right back at you – new flavours and especially textures take some getting used to. The trick is to keep trying and not brand a food as something she doesn't like and never will.

As your baby slowly starts to develop a more recognisable grinding motion with her mouth you can gradually add less liquid to her food and introduce a slightly thicker texture – we're not talking beef wellington here, just soft lumps so your baby can practise her gummy chew and swallow movement and work on those jaw muscles. This will become crucial when talking becomes the next thing on her development menu in a few months' time.

By the time your little one is about seven or eight months old, its recommended that she should be eating mushy solids about three times a day – but do keep an eye out for signs she's full. Just like you or me, some days she'll be hungrier than others and if she refuses to open her mouth, pulls her head away or bangs the high chair and screams 'FOR GOD'S SAKE MAN I'VE HAD ENOUGH!' – she's probably done.

Developing good eating habits from day one is a great idea and can avoid all sorts of fussy eater shenanigans later on, so it's worth offering up a real variety of foods, including deboned fish. You should be avoiding all added salt and sugar for the first year, and it's best to give mega fatty foods the swerve too.

A sip of water from a beaker at mealtimes is also a very good thing. Hard as it may be, try not to get into the habit of using food as a reward or threat – it's very easy to back yourself into a Percy Pig-shaped corner further down the line where just getting out of the front door requires a lorry load of sweets.

Within the wide world of weaning there's been something of a finger food revolution of late. Often termed 'baby-led weaning', it revolves around encouraging babies to feed themselves with safe soft finger foods rather than being spoon-fed. A finger of buttered toast here, a peeled pear there help to promote independence and confidence, and crucially to help to build up your little one's speech muscles right from the off. Finger food is also the cheapest route to an avant-garde redecoration of your kitchen as there is to be found anywhere.

If you go down this route be absolutely sure to stay with your baby when she is feeding herself in case she bites off more than she can chew.

As ever, there's a dazzling array of specialist equipment you can shell out for to help make weaning easier and your wallet lighter, but outside of rubber spoons, a high chair and maybe a suction bowl that will stay put all you need is patience, a sense of humour, and a fluid colour scheme in your home.

There's something very rewarding about watching your baby munching her way through real food, it's a big step and the start of lifelong refueling. A word of warning, though, when your baby starts to eat more like an adult they start to poo more like an adult. Prepare yourself for a change in colour and smell and when meat is introduced to the meal times you'll essentially be changing a baby lion.

Enjoy.

Crawling

As if learning to eat isn't enough of a challenge for your little one to take on, it's highly likely they will also tackle mobility in these few months, too.

There's some evidence that because babies aren't sleeping on their fronts and so strengthening their arms and neck muscles anywhere near as much as they used to, crawling is on its way out. Despite that fact being trotted out a lot by all and sundry, the chances still are you will have a crawler roaming around your living room some time soon.

Crawling may start with your baby balancing on her hands and knees, sometimes accompanied by a comedic rocking back and forth like Usain Bolt on his blocks. Alternatively, you may have a bottom shuffler in the family. This ungainly but surprisingly effective form of transport involves using the backside as the fulcrum and the legs as oar-like appendages.

It might not be a good look, but it works.

Some babies only crawl on hands and feet, others bring their knees into play – in fact it's not the technique that's remotely important, it's getting on the move by hook or by crook that's the big deal. Don't worry if at nine months your baby isn't a speed machine. They are all different. The medical advice is that if they have shown zero interest in moving an inch by the time they are 12 months get them checked out at the GP just in case.

Whenever they do decide to get going you'll need to view your home in a different light – in the words of the legendary consumer broadcaster Lynn Faulds Wood, every nook and cranny is a 'potential death trap'.

All right, that might be a touch alarmist but get down on all fours yourself and have a crawl around. Anything you can swipe, crush, throw or put in your mouth needs moving. Anything you can open, slam, or swing needs securing. Anything you value, even remotely, needs putting at least seven feet off the ground.

'Babyproofing' your house, as it's rather tweely known, is another baby area that has spawned a raft of products and gizmos that will turn your home into a museum of modern plastic if you're not careful.

Some of the kit is vital – try and live without a stairgate and you will be a jabbering, twitching wreck by the end of the week as your baby returns to the forbidden but enticing wooden mountain an astonishing 89 times in a single hour period. You won't talk them out of it, they won't forget, you just need to block it off, no matter how hideous it makes your hall look.

Plug socket blockers, plastic guards for sharp corners, rubber stoppers for heavy doors, clips for forbidden cupboards are all useful too – in fact who am I kidding, the second that you are aware of the existence of a new child safety gadget the pull to buy it is immediately overwhelming. With the Royal Society for the Prevention of Accidents stating that more than 600,000 children aged four or under need hospital treatment each year following accidents in the home, resistance is futile, you'll be urged on by your fear gland to plastic your home to buggery like the rest of us. But it is possible to bypass the babyproofing war, if you choose, by getting your child confident on the first steps under supervision, so that they quickly get a hang of it and a stairgate isn't a necessity.

Apparently the Royal Society for the Pevention of Accidents lists most accidents as happening in the lounge and dining room, closely followed by the kitchen, bathroom and stairs.

There's also research suggesting that most accidents occur during the day, with the hour between 6pm and 7pm being particularly dangerous when meal and bathtime activity is high and energy reserves are low.

So, little did you know it, but the past six months or so have represented a physically less demanding period than the one you now enter. When your baby moves, so do you, and your baby will want to move a lot in all directions.

If you weren't drinking so much red wine the weight would drop off you.

Teething

The way us humans go about getting teeth is on the face of things pretty dumb.

As you are about to discover, milk teeth cause a disproportionate amount of bother in the short time they are operational.

From around the six-month mark onwards, your baby will start the three-year long journey to push out a set of teeth that will give a year or two's service before they start to fall out and are replaced by the real deal.

The process of cutting these baby teeth is termed as eruption by medical folk and never in the field of biological jargon has one word been seen as so apt by so many.

The first series of 10 or so teeth your baby 'cuts' over the next six months have the capability of causing one or all of the following: burning cheeks, red ears, high temperature, broken sleep, an urge to bite everything and everyone within reach, screams of pain as the jagged demon cuts through soft gum, cold-like symptoms, drooling by the bucketful – and nappies so rancid thanks to the acidic teething saliva being produced that you feel like calling in a UN weapons inspection team to give them the all-clear.

Don't put absolutely everything down to teething – and if you are remotely concerned about your baby's behaviour or health, get her checked out with the doctor as soon as you can.

As a loose guide, these eruptions generally start with the central incisors between 6–12 months, then lateral incisors at 9–16 months, first molars 13–19 months, canine teeth at 16–23 months, and second molars at the 22–33 month mark. It's said that tooth development is hereditary so if you gave your folks hell, it's payback time in a big way.

Other than comforting them, there are a few things you can do to relieve the obvious pain many babies go through during teething. Giving them something cold to chew on like a teething ring kept in the fridge works well as does a peeled carrot or slice of chilled apple if they are old enough to chew on it.

You'll see homeopathic teething powder in the chemists and you might as well give it a try. There's next to no evidence it does any good whatsoever but there are parents out there who will wrestle you to the ground rather than concede it's a load of old flowery hokum. At worst they give your teething bub something new to think about for a while once they feel the white granules in their mouth – or should that be a bit of comic relief as they repeatedly push the open packet away leaving you looking like a cack-handed cocaine dealer.

If your baby is older than four months, there are some pretty good gels to rub on their gums – beware once they have already cut the first tooth, they will bite down on you and laugh at your shrieks afterwards.

Then there are the big guns – Calprofen® and Calpol® (infant ibuprofen and paracetamol). Always follow the instructions – and make sure you have some in the house for about the next 20 years.

Words from your fellow fathers

Paul, father of two: *Baby-led weaning might be a bit of a poncy name, but as a strategy it works.*

It's got to be better to let them try all sorts of things in little bits, than to mush everything up into a slop, feed them on that and then suddenly present them with a full roast dinner when they are two and expect them to munch through it.

Marcus, father of four: *Our first baby gave crawling a miss and went straight to walking although we didn't hear the end of it from all the health care professionals.*

Tom, father of two: *Given the midwife described our eldest as a 'lazy boy' for being two weeks overdue, it should have come as no surprise that he was in no hurry to shuffle, let alone walk.*

While frustrating for him (and us when 'other parents' suggested something was wrong) 21 months gave us two summer holidays where he just lay there, which was fairly handy.

As for teething nappies I don't think the word 'rancid' truly does them justice. It's like every bit of evil in the world, popped into a blender and mixed with every bit of road kill, with the whole cocktail placed into a flimsy excuse for a nappy which then channels it all the way up their back.

Nick, father of two: *I'm not sure teeth coming through are the best design. It went on for a week and then you realise that they have 24 of the things and it seems to go on for ever.*

Winston, father of two: *Both mine suffered badly from teething, and your heart goes out to them because it looks so miserable.*

On the plus side, however, teething can be used as an excuse for any sub-par behaviour by your children right up to the age of eight.

Getting to know you

As you slowly emerge blinking into the sunlight from the first six months of parenthood you may well glance to the side and see a figure that you vaguely recognise.

The rounded shoulders, the pallid skin, the 1,000 yard stare, yes they are all familiar, you've passed those features many a time on the pre-dawn landing, trying to block out the distant tweeting of birds as you hunt for the elusive Calpol® syringe like a crazed paracetamol-pushing junkie.

But it's not those traits that are registering with you just now, it's something far more deep-rooted, like an old memory involuntarily twitching back to life in the recesses of your sleep-deprived brain.

This is your partner, the person who just half a year ago was the ying to your yang, the Bonnie to your Clyde, the Janette to your Ian Krankie – and now as you both surface from the baby bunker it's time to start getting to know each other again.

Jetting off to Venice to relight your fire isn't really an option for most – even a trip to the local multiplex involves logistical preparation on a monumental scale. So what do you do to ensure that you don't just turn into a bottle-sterilising, nappy-bin-emptying robotic nightmare of a couple who haven't only forgotten what drove them to have a baby together, but also how they actually managed to make it happen too?

Romance amidst the reflux

It's surprising how hard it is to be warm and loving in the wee small hours of the morning.

Likewise for the ability to retain anything even approaching a sense of humour.

Hysterical laughing, that shows itself from time to time yes, but water off a duck's back, laugh in the face of life's challenges. Bona fide humour? No, not very much of that knocking around at all.

This environment of hard work and fatigue can be stony ground indeed for love's delicate seeds, but there are things you can do, small things, easy things that keep the flame of romance flickering during the tough times, ready for you to take the bellows to it when the time is right.

First of all try, try, try to keep the little intimate gestures that are the understated lifeblood of any relationship going. I'm not talking about a grope that indicates you may have woken up from your slumber enough to feel fruity (we will be getting on to sex shortly). It's the touch as you pass in the kitchen, playing with her hair, giving the poor woman a kiss every now and then. It's vital these aren't meant or seen as a big come-on – having an actual conversation to agree that these little things need to be reintroduced for their own merits is a smart move.

I'm aware this sounds hideously contrived and manufactured but the truth is for a lot of us that unless you work, at least initially, at keeping things ticking over on that front, tiredness and even stress will triumph over love – and we can't have that, can we?

As we've already acknowledged the long weekend away is a big, big ask just now – if breastfeeding is still going on it's almost definitely out unless your partner is an expressing queen. Even when bottlefeeding is the route of choice, many new parents find handing their baby over to even the most trusted and experienced friend or relative incredibly hard to do for more than a night.

But an afternoon or an evening out will do you more good than you can imagine. You might be checking the phone a lot to see if all is well, but getting away, properly away to a nice restaurant or for a film and a pizza is crucial. Don't put it off, organise it now and make it happen, it doesn't have to be flash. Pooh sticks on the river and a picnic will do – you'll be glad you did.

When you've done it the once and the world didn't end, get another date in the diary pronto. It doesn't have to be that soon even, the anticipation of a break can get you both through all sorts of trials.

You're the entertainment officer now as well as the daddy, so crack on.

By the way, don't for a moment think I'm suggesting all this as someone who knows all the answers – my wife will be reading this to a soundtrack of derisive shrieks that will be knocking pictures off walls. No, most of this wisdom is pieced together from the dads I've spoken to, all of whom made mistakes galore, but between them were nestled some real gems to help insulate your relationship in the tough times.

Choosing to spend hours on end writing a book in the first years of parenthood probably wasn't one of them if I'm honest though.

Sex and the newly parented

At the heart of the altered relationship arena for new parents is, of course, sex.

Depending on your respective sex drives, the often-decreasing amount of lovemaking you find the time for can cause obvious and profound problems for how together you feel as a couple and how able you are to cope with all that your new life will throw at you.

In a nutshell, the closer you feel the more intimate you'll be with each other, the more intimate you are with each other the better able to cope and be tolerant and sympathetic with each other you'll be – and the closer you'll feel.

Catch that number 22.

While it's often the case that the man wants sex and the woman not so much, as with all generalisations there are many, many cases where the opposite is true. Pressure at work and at home may mean the very last thing you feel capable of is performing in the bedroom big top.

Whatever your particular configuration though, there will need to be, at some point, the first time you make love since baby was born.

Official medical advice suggests around eight weeks or so. For many women the sheer physical upheaval that they have endured is enough to lengthen that time frame by some considerable distance, not to mention how absolutely exhausted the adults in the household are too.

Whenever you both decide to reacquaint yourselves, it's worth remembering that in many ways it's very much like the first time all over again and you'll need to take it nice and slow.

Without getting too graphic, women can be a bit dry during sex, especially if they are breastfeeding. So don't get upset and think she's not turned on, have some personal lubricant to hand and let her chose the position and pace that's right. Also be prepared for things to feel a bit different too – there's been a lot going on down there.

That was quite graphic actually wasn't it – it's best to know, though.

A word of warning: Don't be fooled into thinking that you can do without birth control for a nice long while – it's true that a woman isn't fertile immediately after birth, especially if she's breastfeeding, but guessing how long that spell will last is a game of Russian Roulette you'll not want to lose, unless you are immediately ready for number two (are you mad?). The hormones in most oral contraceptives don't mix with breastfeeding either, so you are looking at some sort of barrier method too – always nice.

As well as the physical elements that make up being ready for bedroom intimacy there's the emotional side, too. There's many a reason why more time and understanding might be needed. Your partner may be seriously apprehensive about pain, she may not feel at her most physically attractive, after the indignity of labour she may not feel quite the same about her most intimate parts for a while and she will definitely be knackered beyond belief.

Space, affection, understanding and compliments are the order of the day – applying even delicate pressure may well start a chain of events which will turn sex into a battleground and bargaining chip – which is deeply unsexy and unfulfilling for everyone involved.

You wouldn't do that, would you?

Your partner may not be the only one who has a few mental scars that need to heal either. Some men have real trouble recovering from the sights they viewed during the labour, especially the gynaecologically graphic moments. As with all these psychological issues the romancing and the wooing we've already talked about is the way to go. You're both going through an enthralling but exhausting time of your lives where you are essentially falling in love with the new little person in your lives while your partner's body and hormones are still on a massive come-down.

It's tough, so if you can, give yourselves a break and enjoy getting to know each other again.

Words from your fellow fathers

Nick, father of two: *I think our first overnighter without the baby was at a wedding.*

We completely over played our hand, as though the world might never serve us alcohol again, if we didn't show some form.

Regretted that, until the next time.

Stuart, father of two: *We didn't have family close by and didn't know any babysitters we could trust so I think our first night out was months if not over a year after our eldest was born.*

As for an overnighter together with no kids – we're still waiting for that to happen four years in!

Tom, father of two: *Put it this way, I never ever in a million years, thought I'd hear myself saying I'm too tired.*

Paul, father of two: *Sleep is the new sex.*

Your progress report

Your baby

Given that your clever little tot is learning to crawl, eating solid food and cutting teeth during this three-month spell, you'd imagine she'd have very little time for much else.

Not a bit of it! She is a learning machine, and among other things you might find that she starts to turn towards you when she hears her own name. When you stop to think about that, it is an astonishing achievement. Not only is she picking up that the noises people make mean something, she has even associated one of the thousands of slightly different sounds she has heard so far in her brief life with being something to do with her.

She's a genius. They all are.

She'll also start to imitate you, nodding, shaking her head, sticking her tongue out. The beginnings of an independent spirit – more of which in the next chapter – start to shine through as she grabs at her bottle or spoon and attempts to feed herself.

Peek-a-boo will start to be the most entertaining pastime your household has ever seen at this stage, and it will retain its popularity for months to come.

If you've not taken your little one swimming yet get your trunks on. Getting your baby used to water early doors makes an awful lot of sense from a safety point of view and they have an absolute ball in the water.

You'll need to ensure you have a tonne of kit in the swim bag from swim nappies and toys, to a snack and the ubiquitous changing mat – but it's well worth the rigmarole to see her little face as she splashes around and enjoys a real sense of freedom as she is surrounded by liquid, just like she was less than a year ago!

Your partner

If your partner is still breastfeeding, you may well have to become accustomed to blood-curdling screams from her as your recently betoothed baby bites down on her nipple.

Yikes!

Looking after a baby who moves is unsurprisingly a lot more shattering than keeping an eye on one who helpfully stays exactly where you plonk them. Even when you are in the same room as them the average length of any sit down you may sneak would be, should any academics have measured it, no more than 15 seconds in length, I'll wager.

All of which goes to create a very, very tired person who greets you, often with baby in outstretched arms, as you return from work. If you've still not reached a state of 'sleeping through' yet then we are talking some serious fatigue here and you'll have to play a big part in helping run the house and keeping your partner's pecker up.

You

The only trouble with the last sentence above is that you'll be pretty knackered, too – which can lead to some rather fractious conversations.

The classic battleground on this front is the fact that after a long hard day at work you come home and naturally feel the need to relax and unwind. Your partner, after a day feeding, chasing and cleaning a teething, crawling, yoghurt-throwing nipper sees your entrance through the front door as her long awaited chance to relax and unwind.

There's a problem there, isn't there? – but what's the answer?

Please do let me and the rest of parentkind know if you happen to stumble across it.

What's for sure is that clear, unemotional communication can really help avoid flash points and arguments that make already difficult situations much, much worse. In some ways, *when* to raise an issue is almost more important than *how* you do it. Choosing a peaceful, relatively calm moment to discuss something, whether that be about the division of labour, childcare techniques or whatever, is infinitely preferable to letting your hackles get the best of you and spewing out a long list of pent-up frustrations right in the middle of an already stressful moment.

Once you've got things off your chest at the least inflammatory moment possible you'll need a cocktail of compromise, understanding and humility topped up with copious amounts of humour to make a new plan and move on.

MONTHS 10-12

You've come a long way, baby

Pretty soon you'll have been a father for an entire year.

Although you may feel you've aged 10 times that amount and that you've never worked so hard, worried so much or slept so little – the chances are it will shock you just how quickly time has passed and how much your floppy newborn has changed in these 12 months.

As if to rub it in technically the term 'baby' no longer applies past the first year – you've got an 'infant' on your hands from this point onwards – although no doubt your baby will be called 'your baby' for many years to come yet.

As well as deciding how best to celebrate the year milestone this spell may well also see your little one take an enormous evolutionary step in every sense of the word, as she casts aside her recently acquired skill of crawling in favour of walking.

The development of physical independence is also matched by the mental and emotional strides taken now, too. A real sense of self often becomes apparent and with that comes a sense of others – you and your partner in particular. In a beautifully choreographed piece of psychological learning your baby can almost at a stroke become more *independent* as she gets to know herself and at the same time more *dependent* as her recognition of both of you leads to separation anxiety if and when you have to be apart – or even if one of you merely leaves the room.

Separation can be a hot topic for mothers, too, during these few months. Maternity leave often ends for many, with the readjustment back to work and – perhaps more dauntingly – the childcare conundrum all to be tackled.

Meanwhile your baby is as cute as a button in what is a glorious stage of her young life as she continues to explore, grow in confidence and melt your heart with her ever-widening smile.

Walking

Learning to walk isn't just one of the most impressive things your baby will ever do, it isn't just a huge leap towards independence. It is an anthropological, evolutionary marvel and it'll probably happen right in your front room.

After just 12 months or so on the planet the new little human in your house will be desperate to get in on the act, too.

It's natural, almost inevitable that you'll get a bit twitchy when one of your baby's contemporaries makes one giant leap before your pride and joy does. As the comedian Michael McIntyre wryly points out, you don't often see adults dragging themselves into work because they just never got round to learning the walking thing – so try and relax, if your baby is otherwise physically healthy, it will happen.

Once she moves from crawling to pulling herself up on the furniture and cruising around the joint, it's only a matter of time and confidence. By around the 15-month mark most healthy babies are walking on their own, so have a little patience. Luxuriate in the knowledge that once they do start marching around the place they are even more of a handful until they really master their steps months later.

From cruising they can move into the clean and jerk where they slowly squat and stand, squat and stand like a lethargic Cossack dancer. Then it's often on to the 'look at me' holding hands stage where with your help they motor around the place sporting an almightily cute grin.

From there they will gradually pluck up the courage to take that first step on their own. While it would be fantastic if it were to happen in front of the two of you with various camcorders and a lighting rig set up, don't be too crestfallen if it's just your partner or the childminder or nursery staff who get the privilege of witnessing the golden moment. Just be grateful and proud she has cracked it and know that you have played a massive part in helping her reach that milestone, and every other one along the way, too.

You can certainly help your baby along the way and the toddle truck toys you see are great for encouraging them, although you'll need to be standing nearby for a while. Before you know it, you'll be happily chopping an onion when your lower ankle will be rammed at high speed in a surprise attack.

Baby walkers, the proto Dalek-wheeled chariot that were all the rage a decade ago, have seriously fallen out of favour and are even banned in some countries – it's argued that as well as giving your baby extra height to get at hitherto out of reach danger items on work tops, they can adversely affect your baby's development.

Likewise, baby bouncers that hang from door frames have also become frowned upon. The best bet is to Google them both and read up on the pros and cons before you make your mind up.

As your baby learns to walk, it's best not to truss her feet up in shoes too soon. It's not as if she will be walking on shingle at this stage and the more chance her feet have to grow unfettered, the better. Once she is ready for the great outdoors a qualified fitter is recommended – despite the fact that gram for gram, baby shoes must be the most expensive item on the planet outside of weapons-grade plutonium.

If your baby seems to be really lagging behind and isn't walking by around 18 months, go and see your GP. They'll do some blood tests, to rule out any rare muscle disorders. They say the chances are that if you or your partner were particularly late walkers your children could be too, so a word with the folks could reassure you – or make things a hundred times worse, depending what they are like – bloody parents eh?

Words from your fellow fathers

Paul, father of two: *Both of mine have taken their first steps at their grandparents' house. This is either because despite being OAPs they have the energy to cajole it out of them or the fact that they have lovely soft carpet and we have practical, wipe-clean floorboards.*

Mark, father of one: *I missed the first steps but she did them again for me when I came back from work.*
It was truly moving and funny seeing her get some independence but then do a funny waddle across the room.

Winston, father of two: *I might not have seen the very first steps, but certainly among the first.*
The look of achievement on her face was something to behold.

Independence days

Here's a strange thing to consider. It's believed that when your baby is a newborn she thinks she's a part of her mother and, to a lesser degree, you. You only have to watch the look of bemusement bordering on terror when she first discovers her own arms and hands (at around four months) to know that's the case.

As her fleshy appendages flail around in front of her their eyes widen as if she's being teased by a giant squid – if I'm you Mum, who the hell owns these two things?

At around six months of life, the penny drops and she'll start to realise that she is a person in her own right. Quite how mindblowing that moment of clarity must be is almost beyond comprehension and it's arguable that as humans we never make a discovery as profound ever again.

Once you realise that you are you and not someone else, the next step is to realise that if you're not particularly liking something, or would rather it done another way – your way – kicking off about it is most definitely an option. This sense of individuality which slowly begins to develop now takes years to develop fully, but what you begin to see now are the seeds of the toddler tantrums you'll encounter soon and also a glimpse into your child's broader personality.

Which is both exciting and fascinating.

The other side of the independence coin is realising that you can be apart from others and separation anxiety also kicks in around this time, too.

Separation anxiety

Up until the six- or seven-month mark your baby hasn't got time for psycho codswallop like developing a sense of self – she is a survival machine, food and love are what she needs and everything else can form an orderly queue behind Mummy.

But gradually as she discovers that she can do things like smile and get smiles back, cry for attention and get angry at the unspeakable injustices heaped upon her like nappy changing and face washing, she learns that what she does affects these two people who seem to be hanging around a lot, which must mean that she is separate from them.

What a clever little baby.

It's around this point of enlightenment that you'll likely start to notice that either of you, but especially your partner leaving the room will often result in a sudden bout of tears. Trouble is, she doesn't yet realise that when you nip to the loo, you'll be back.

Sneaking out so she doesn't see you leave isn't advisable, according to some child psychologists (although you may well find yourself instinctively doing it to avoid upset) because it can make her even more afraid when she suddenly notices you've gone.

Interestingly games like peek-a-boo and later hide-and-seek can help develop an understanding of separation and return. If you disappear under a blanket and then come back you'll do the same when you leave the room or the house. The reason she laughs at peek-a-boo is because the laugh and the cry are very close bedfellows, indeed even in adults – the scream on the rollercoaster is perhaps the absolute middle ground between the two, titillation and excitement when fear of the unknown is close at hand.

Your baby might still be getting upset at being left at nursery when she is two or more so this is a long-term process. What's vital is that throughout it she is becoming slowly more secure, more content that you will come back. This trust is built up by the love and care you show for her. As her memory develops, she taps into that more and more in her moments of anxiety when one or both of you aren't there.

This is pretty deep-rooted stuff and you can see as clear as day how a repeatedly insecure existence at this tender age can have major implications later down the line. What's equally important is that you don't castigate yourselves for having to go to work – it's a fact of life in our society where a single income often doesn't even come close to covering a mortgage.

What's also a fact of life is that children absolutely need to develop a strong sense of independence and be secure enough to step out on their own. As ever in parenthood, especially when both parents work, it's about striking a tricky balance between keeping your children safe and letting them explore, running a household and spending time with your children, comforting them and keeping them close while encouraging them to develop and learn on their own.

In many ways, this is one of the most central challenges any parent ever faces and it's true to say men and women approach it differently. Just as it's been noted that women tend to hold their youngsters into them to protect and men outwards so they can observe, both you and your partner will bring different skills to the table where independence and separation is concerned. You may allow them to take a few more supervised risks or, on the flip side, become more impatient further down the line when they seek comfort when you may think they should pick themselves up and dust themselves off.

Both approaches are valid and needed, it's down to you and your partner to create the right blend of the two for your child – and that blending starts now.

Within all of this, what is irrefutable is that your baby and later toddler needs a rock solid attachment to you and your partner so that she can begin to explore the world securely and test her developing skills – safe in the knowledge that she can always return to you.

Giving her consistent love, engagement and confidence-building encouragement is key to creating that attachment, that trust. As your baby moves into toddlerhood, ensuring there is a safe environment for her to explore at home is also a key factor meaning she won't constantly hear 'no' when she is trying to strike out and learn.

Later on, when she is striding forth ready to take on the world as a three-, four- or five-year-old, she will still need to know that you are there when needed, uncritical, loving and warm. When you think about your relationship with your own parents as I've just done writing that, the need for that safe haven from the people who were there in your most formative years never really fully leaves us does it?

With all that in mind, it's obvious to see why providing your child with the best possible environment when you can't be with them at this early stage in their lives becomes such an all-consuming issue for parents everywhere.

Work and the modern family: welcome to the childcare carnival

Across the globe more mothers than ever before are working – and nowhere is this trend more prevalent than here in the UK.

Half of British mums go back to work before their child's first birthday, according to a worldwide report in 2011 by the Organisation for Economic Co-operation and Development (OECD) – with more than a quarter of them in paid work before their child is six months old.[10]

The same research, which focussed on the world's leading 34 industrialised nations, also suggested that this new reality of the working mum could be having negative impact on child development, with 'serious effects on behaviour and attention spans by the time the child is seven' cited, with the impact becoming greater the earlier the return to work.

While taking great care to avoid an alarmist 'we're all doomed' reaction to the domestic pattern many parents find themselves in nowadays, it does throw up many a question – the main one being, have we all, but especially today's women, been sold a lie?

It feels, in many ways, that governmental obsession with economic growth and the untethered, invisible and rampant hand of the free market have combined to hijack the green shoots of feminism and promise today's women that they can 'have it all' – the family, the career, the house, the car, the husband, the fondue set, the lot.

All they need to do to make it happen, these ultra-dynamic daughters of the new dawn, is find another eight hours in each and every day and they will be home and hosed.

Failure to pull off this time trick leaves your partner often facing a barrage of accusatory and guilt inducing headlines – Working Mums Make Kids Fat, Working Mothers Have Sicker Children, Working Mums Look After Kids for Just 80 Minutes A Day – the studies and the stories keep on coming and the pressure keeps on mounting.

So what's the answer – and what can you do to help make things better?

Aside from earning/finding/stealing a wedge of money so thick it renders all options permanently open, it's an intractable issue that has become even more of a headache now that the consumer-driven capitalist model which promised us Westerners most sincerely that if we worked all the hours God sends we could all live the dream, is looking very, very poorly indeed.

When you consider that in 1968 only 18% of women earned the same or more than their male partners and that today that is the case in 44% of households you can see just how integral woman's earning power has become to both the national and domestic purse.

This profound shift in the economic fabric has led to the rise in the stay-at-home dad, with a recent survey suggesting that the number of fathers acting as the primary carer now stands at around 600,000   a tenfold increase over the last decade.[11]

With the introduction of plans to turn maternity leave into joint leave that can be shared between both parents, even more fathers will be able to spend time with their children. The stay-at-home dad may become a permanent fixture in our society and an increasingly large and vociferous group capable of making its own views known.

Anyone like me who has had a spell as the main carer will know that there is still a little way to go before that happens though. Walking into a play group or a one o'clock club as a man can still feel somewhat akin to sitting in the away end with the wrong scarf on.

All right, so there's no abuse given and orchestrated chanting is very rarely encountered but for every lovely open, brave mum who will come over and chat there are a good few whose suspicions result in the cold shoulder being given, perhaps subconsciously, as you transgress on what has hitherto been an all-female domain.

All that will change in the months and years to come of course as dads become less of a rarity on the baby and toddler circuit. The househusband will be seen not as a figure of fun but more of a parental force to be reckoned with.

Go boyfriends!

Childcare

Plenty of parents are more than happy with a situation which allows them to both achieve fulfillment through their respective careers while enjoying a family too.

There are also those who post-maternity/paternity leave would love nothing more than to spend some or all of the week with their young ones, but whose finances dictate that they both need to work every hour they can just to keep the wolf from the door.

What these groups share is a reliance on childcare in some shape or form – and, as you may have already found out, this is an incredibly expensive and complex area. The OECD report mentioned earlier went as far as to say that quality childcare in the UK was among the most expensive in the Western world. In fact it's a multibillion pound industry in the UK and with a number of options open to parents there's a lot to get your head around.

Childminders

Childminders have become a hugely popular childcare option over the past 20 years or so, with registered childminders being regulated by Ofsted in England and the relevant bodies in Scotland, Wales and Northern Ireland, to look after babies and older children.

As well as the Ofsted checks, which mean that they must attend a registration and first aid course within six months of enlisting, all childminders must be Criminal Records Bureau (CRB) checked, as must all adult members of their family who share their home.

In the main children are looked after at the childminder's home, which itself has to be inspected regularly by Ofsted, but some can offer their services based in your home rather than theirs.

Finding a childminder you, your partner and your child likes is vital and tricky in equal measure. You need to seek someone out who has a good reputation, can deal equally with their own children, if they have any, and those in their care and can be firm and fair without scaring the bejesus out of either you or your kids.

It goes without saying that a childminder who doesn't enjoy being with children is to be avoided as is someone who you sense will reach for the TV remote the moment they need to keep the kids occupied. As with all childminding options, the chances are your little ones will be spending some serious time in the company of this person and if they have some creative ways to engage their happy gaggle everyone will benefit.

Knowing that your tot is being looked after in a warm friendly home by someone you trust and like is worth an awful lot – which is precisely what you'll be paying for it.

Nurseries

Nurseries employ a combination of qualified and unqualified staff to look after children from as young as four months old up to five years of age.

Open for anything up to 11 hours per day the modern nursery works hard to accommodate parents' work situations and although many close for a short break in the summer they tend to be open pretty much across the board.

Choosing a nursery takes time and asking around in the local area even before you have children can be very worthwhile as many places at the best nurseries are booked up months in advance. The average nursery place will set you back £113 a week so it's reckoned, but you can easily find yourself paying much, much more, with prices reaching £300 per week not unheard of.

·Less intimate than the childminder or nanny option what they do offer is a real sense of socialisation for your little one, if that's what you think they will need and thrive on.

Nannies

For the most part when people say they have a nanny they have an arrangement with someone who looks after their children in their own home, has a recognised childcare qualification and is responsible for duties including planning activities, assisting in the child's development, shopping for and preparing the youngster's meals, keeping the child's areas of the house clean and tidy and doing the child's laundry.

That's quite a list and even more of a responsibility.

Nannies are an attractive option for many who can afford them – as well as offering one-to-one care, the disruption to your child's routine is minimised because the care takes place for the most part in the familiar surroundings of your home.

If you've ever seen Mary Poppins, you'll know all too well that finding the right nanny is a tricky and time-consuming business. Notwithstanding having your ideal candidate floating in on an umbrella you'll have to place ads, use agencies and keep your ear to the ground to able to snare the right one for you and your family.

The cost?

Well before we talk about anything as grubby as money bear in mind that when you hire a nanny you become an employer. It's down to you to sort out paying tax and National Insurance and then there's sick and holiday pay.

And what perks can you offer? Use of the car, private health care, gym membership? We might be looking toward the top end with these kind of sweeteners but increasingly the market is becoming a cut-throat world – which is why the average nanny takes home between £258 and £328 a week with supercalifragilistic ones pocketing much, much more than that.

Au pairs

I have news. Au pairs exist in real life and not just in 70s sitcoms.

An au pair is a foreign national who in exchange for the opportunity to learn another language and a spot of board and lodging at your place will do some housework and childcare duties.

Most au pairs aren't strictly trained in childcare and most agencies who hook them up with prospective parents suggest that they are best used for older children, but the prospect of an au pair to help around the house, babysit and look after the children during the day has its obvious appeal. But things can and do on occasion go a bit pear shaped.

The language barrier might be too much, the lack of genuine childcare experience and training may not sit well with you in reality, perhaps you'll go power mad and ask them to do way too much or maybe they just won't fit in with family life in your house for one of a million reasons.

Whatever the reason may be, because there is no real contract as such they can simply leave without notice if they wish. The agency can often help resolve some of these issues, but it's important not to be blinded by the benefits of an au pair and ignore the potential pitfalls.

Financially, au pairs offer serious value for money. They are generally expected to work for five days a week, up to a maximum of five hours per day and be available to babysit for two nights a week.

It's good, ya?

Family members

Despite the proliferation in other childcare options, informal arrangements with relatives still make up most childcare arrangements in the UK.

Whether it's reciprocal arrangements between two related part-time workers or a mother/mother-in-law tag team of fearsome proportions, family members can offer low or no cost, flexible and ultra-secure childcare, just as they have for millennia.

As well as the obvious positives there are some equally obvious pitfalls too.

'Mum, we'd just like a word about the knife-throwing game you are playing with them.'

Just as going into business with a relative can be a recipe for unhappy families, so childcare can generate some intergenerational heat when it comes to delivering friendly tips and suggestions.

But if you've got a relative with whom you have a good honest relationship and who shares your general philosophy on bringing up children, then as well as being quids in and a lucky bugger you will also be giving your child perhaps the most loving and secure childcare option of them all.

Flexible working

As well as carefully choosing which childcare route works best for you, your partner and your infant, there are two things you can try to wheedle out of your employers which could help in different ways.

Flexible working is simply the act of finding a way of working which suits both you and your employer.

Whoever set up the whole Monday to Friday nine to five thing obviously didn't have a daily school run to squeeze in, so increasingly flexible working patterns are being agreed across a range of industries ranging from part-time working, to flexi-time days or job shares.

What's more, you, as a father, are just as entitled to have a flexible working request considered as mothers are. If it's refused, there must be valid reasons for saying no – 'Don't be daft, you're a man' won't cut it.

So, if you have a child under the age of six and have been employed for six months by the time you apply, you can put in a serious request and expect serious consideration – the trick is to do some real planning and research before you put your request together. Are there any other fathers and mothers who have had flexible working sanctioned where you work? If so, how? What could your employer's objections be and how can you mitigate against them?

Also make sure you put some effort into your presentation and show your boss that you've not only taken this very seriously, but that it also means a great deal to you. On your part you need to be sure that if as part of your plan you are suggesting a drop in hours you can really cope with the subsequent drop in salary. Trying to undo it can be very tricky.

But if you are sure you can cope financially, flexible working can be a real bonus for you and your partner and as well as potentially reducing your childcare bill you can get to spend some proper time with your child during the week, rather than flying in the door at five to seven only to find you've missed bathtime again.

Childcare vouchers

Equally as helpful, although nowhere near as exciting, are childcare voucher schemes. These allow you to ring-fence a stipulated part of your salary to pay for childcare. You don't pay tax or National Insurance on that slice of what you earn, so you get more bang for your buck and can save hundreds of pounds a year.

Your employer needs to be signed up to the scheme for you to be able to benefit, but if they're not, point out to them that it also means they can reduce the size of their payroll costs and increase staff satisfaction levels to boot.

If that doesn't work, erect a tented village outside the Human Resources director's office until they capitulate.

....

Words from your fellow fathers

Nick, father of two: *We tried an au pair. She was terrible.*

We knew it was bad when our boy would walk in the room and just look at his shoes when she was there. She ended up sleeping in our bed when we went away for a weekend. She left soon afterwards.

My wife is freelance and we found this great woman who is really flexible, the children love and can turn up at the drop of a hat. If not we begged grandparents.

Colin, father of two: *We were lucky – we found a childminder a minute away from my wife's work and she was flexible so when I wasn't working we didn't have to pay for childcare and I could look after our daughter.*

Ben, father of two: *Find a very earnest friend who has a slightly older child than you who has vetted all the local nurseries first and then just copy them.*

Stuart, father of two: *As soon as we got pregnant we knew that once my partner's maternity leave was up I would leave my job as a graphic designer (as I could continue doing little jobs from home) and become a stay-at-home dad. So from our point of view it was pretty straightforward.*

Baby is One!

Congratulations! An entire year has passed since you first became a dad and you have survived – let's celebrate.

In all honesty your baby's first birthday is more for you and your partner than it is for your little one – and there's nothing wrong with that is there?

Negotiating the first year is something you should be rightly proud of because between the three of you an awful lot has been learnt. Tears have been shed, foul smells have been emitted and the occasional smile has been coaxed with a tickle here and there.

But it's not all about you – what do you give to the one-year-old who has everything, if by everything you mean an old telly remote and half a biscuit from under the high chair?

The answer is that presents don't matter a jot, the chances are she's already inundated with plastic toys that are magnetically attracted to the underside of your feet the minute the lights are off. The best present they could get is you having a day off work and playing on the carpet with them for five hours solid.

Another good thing to do is take a picture on the big day and then on each birthday subsequently. As well as being a really lovely memento and memory jogger (the amount you seem to forget as a parent and the speed at which you forget it never fails to amaze and disturb me) it will also act as ideal embarrassment fodder should you wish to plaster the entire reception venue with them when their wedding comes around.

But if a shed load of presents is a waste of cash, a party, a gathering, a get together, a shindig, a bit of a do, most certainly isn't – you all deserve it!

Party time

As we've seen, one-year-olds aren't necessarily the biggest socialisers in the world. The guest list, if they were in charge, might just about stretch to mum, dad, grandparents. . .and, er. . .that's it. A houseful of strange faces all chanting a weird song at you while flashing lights go off and tiny sticks are set on fire sounds like something that just missed the final cut of the *Wicker Man*. If you get carried away and plan too big, you could well have a tearful tot on your hands.

Some youngsters love other babies, others couldn't be more indifferent towards them if they wore a jumper saying 'DO I KNOW YOU?' – so it's down to you and your partner to set the level just right. The antenatal class crowd is often a good bet, with joint parties a good option given the proximity of the birthdays, or maybe just keep it to a bit of a family do?

A couple of hours for the kids is way long enough, but if you want to make it a bit of a let-your-hair-down session for all the parents in the house, make sure you do your maths and take naps into account to avoid a cacophony of cries drowning out the sound of popping corks.

Cake? Of course.

Party bags? Give yourselves a break.

Theme? Absolutely not.

Restock the changing table? Good idea

Double check stairgates? You bet your ass.

No matter how small you make this party, you will be a busy boy, guaranteed. So it's a good idea to get someone else to take pictures and videos. Also try not to fall out because 'someone' forgot to put the bubbly in the fridge or any of a list of other trivial occurrences that will almost certainly happen – it doesn't matter, it's your baby's first birthday!

At the end of the day, when the house is quiet, the cake has been trodden firmly into the carpet and the cat has been peeled off the ceiling, make sure you share a glass of something nice (it'll be cold by now!) with your partner, take a look at the pictures from the day and even a few from the year you've just completed together and toast yourselves – you did it.

Words from your fellow fathers

Ben, father of two: *Kept it all very low key. Small family tea party. Only mentalists and very rich stay-at-home mums have big parties before children are three and even then they ALWAYS end in tears.*

Jason, father of two: *We had the two families round. Could have been disastrous but went quite well. Babies do positive things.*

Winston, father of two: *We had lots of family, mums and dads and babies and my daughter cried when everyone sang* Happy Birthday *because she didn't like the tune.*
You want to celebrate for getting through it and we ended up pissed as loons at the end.

Simon, father of one: *Coincidentally, our son shares his birthday with my Dad, so we had a joint celebration. Low key – a few friends and family, a few beers, a few rows.*

Your progress report

Your baby

Your standing, cruising and potentially walking miracle of a baby can also start to develop a taste for some very light rough play around now.

It's a funny thing, rough play. On one hand it's as stereotypical as it gets, exactly what people would expect a lumbering dad to do with their delicate and precious babies – spin them around a bit in an oafish display of chimp-like exuberance. But guess what, in the last few years research has started to unearth just how important the more roughhouse type of play is in young children's development.

At this tender age the utmost care must be taken when playing. Oversized heads and still under-strength necks must be treated

with absolute caution, but it's at about this time that you and your little one will begin a physical interaction that will carry on for many years and according to scientists at the University of Newcastle in Australia, deliver some profound benefits.

The researchers believe that this kind of play creates a sense of achievement when the child 'defeats' a more powerful adult, which in turn builds their self-confidence and concentration.

As well as letting them win though, when dads resist their children in rough play the crucial lesson that we don't always triumph in life is also communicated in a powerful and real way. The researchers even went on to suggest that the very act of a stronger adult holding back that strength also helps to build deep-rooted trust between father and child.

So maybe the apes know what they are doing after all?

You might also start to notice the beginnings of a vocabulary at this stage, the 'da-das' and 'ma-mas' might be more detectable, and there might even be an odd ow or a meow knocking about too. In the next chapter we will look at how your baby learns in such a scarily impressive way.

Your partner

The end of the first year can be a tough time for your partner – it may be the point she stops breastfeeding, goes back to work or both. Together with your baby walking and even starting to talk, all this can culminate in a real sense of time passing incredibly quickly, of your little one growing up before your eyes.

Luckily your partner will still be so exhausted that any feelings of loss or wistfulness will be edged out by bone crunching fatigue and a constant worry that the last person who went up the stairs (you) didn't close the gate.

She might not have lost all the weight she wanted, she may not be able to remember the days when going to bed at 8.30 on a Saturday night would have seemed sad rather than exciting and she may never have thought that having an uninterrupted shower would seem the very height of luxury – but your partner has been a mum for a whole year and she's changed and grown in ways she never dreamed possible.

A little gift for her to celebrate what she has achieved in these past 12 months would be, I'm sure you'd agree, richly deserved, not to mention going down really rather well.

You

Then there's you. Did the things you were worried about before the baby arrive pan out, or where you broadsided by stuff that simply hadn't occurred to you?

Has your new role as a father made a difference to the way you view the job you do to earn money, or has your position as family breadwinner simply added on even more pressure to bring home the bacon?

Have you developed a new appreciation or understanding for your own father, or have the strength of your new found paternal feelings simply generated more questions in your mind about the relationship you have with him?

Being a dad brings some serious emotional stuff to the surface on a regular basis. While it's tempting to beat it back down again with the thick end of a packet of wet wipes, if you can air some of it with your partner you will reap the benefits on all sorts of levels.

There's much more to come, when your toddler tries your patience and you feel anger towards them for the first time. When someone else's child is mean or even violent towards your little angel you'll be tested – my, how you'll be tested – but you can handle it, grow from it even, because along with the trials will come moments of joy and pride that will swell your chest to bursting point.

But for now, let's just say well done on the first year and assume the brace position for toddlerhood.

YEAR 2

MONTHS 13-16

Your baby: the information junkie

Your baby enters her second year having learnt to smile, interact, eat, move and make your heart disintegrate with the merest wave of the hand or point of the finger.

Chances are she will also be starting to turn her babbling into the basis of coherent words. As she sits in the high chair and fixes you in her cheeky gaze you might find that the traditional dropping of the broccoli floret on the floor will be accompanied by a beautifully delivered 'Uh oh'.

This is seriously impressive stuff, but just you wait, she's only just beginning and will soon start to pick up words, intonation and expression at a frightening rate. Before you know where you are you'll have a three-year-old who sits in the back of the car and asks if you are lost, when you frankly have no idea where you are. But just how do they do it? How do they suck up information so quickly given that adulthood renders the remembering of more than one password for your laptop all but an impossibility?

What's more, what can you do to encourage, facilitate and help them learn without turning into the kind of 'show them how you can count to 50 in French' parent you have always wanted to resist becoming?

What toys are best to buy? Is putting them in front of the TV even remotely educational or is it simply the only way you know to buy the time needed to empty the dishwasher?

There are many more questions too, some of them so new that finding answers to them is tough – notably around the digital revolution we are in the midst of – do iPhone apps teach them anything or just make your car journey easier? Should you encourage them to use a computer or discourage it and get a Victorian spinning top out?

As you may imagine, hard and fast rules are thin on the ground, but these are all issues that will run and run throughout your parenting career and you'll be amazed at how quickly you are forced to address them. All the evidence, as we will see, points to the fact that the earlier you get a handle on things in this realm as a parent, the more your child will benefit.

The reality is, your infant, not even 18 months old yet, will almost certainly be irresistibly drawn to not just books, but the goggle box in the corner of the room and any digital device they see you using. Then it's only a matter of time before they will make you look like a leaden-fingered luddite as they master them in ways you never knew existed.

Let's start this journey by looking at how your baby's brain manages to pull the great learning trick off.

How babies learn

It's pretty clear that the first three years of life are a period of incredible and never-to-be-repeated growth and development.

At birth, a baby's brain is about 25% of its approximate adult weight, but by the age of three it has spurted in dramatic fashion and produced billions of cells and trillions of communication routes called synapses that link the cells together and form the network of all networks. This makes the internet look as complex and technically impressive as a pushbike in comparison.

While it's true that the young brain's development takes years to complete and indeed that our grey matter shapes and reshapes itself throughout our lives to adapt and cope with new challenges and experiences, it's becoming increasingly clear that what youngsters encounter and engage with from the very start of their existence has a huge part to play in laying the right foundations for learning right through their lives.

What's more, what a child experiences in its early days profoundly influences how that development will take place and the way they interact with the world throughout their lives.

They might not to be able to remember a single thing you've done for them in these early years and months but, my goodness, it will have an effect on them.

According to the World Health Organization, a startling array of challenges in adulthood, like mental health issues, obesity, heart disease, criminality as well as the perhaps more obvious instances of poor literacy and numeracy, can be traced back to early childhood and the environment children learn from.[12]

In the relatively recent past extended family members were often close by, offering us advice and being the role models for us newbie parents – but with the change in the way we live and work, that isn't the case for a growing number of us anymore.

Which all amounts to the reality that as if keeping them away from the stairs, out of the fire and off the M6 wasn't responsibility enough, you and your partner are also very much in charge of the brain department, too.

Perhaps the most stark way your baby's experiences shape their brain growth is the way in which they learn language.

Language and literacy

By the time an infant is just three months old her brain can distinguish several hundred different spoken sounds rather than words; that's comfortably more than exist in her native language.

As the months move on, though, she will filter out the sounds she doesn't need and recognise only those that are part of the language she regularly hears. The brain doesn't discard this astonishing skill completely though, oh no, during early childhood it stores the ability to re-learn sounds it has discarded at the drop of a linguist hat.

This smart move explains why young children typically learn new languages in a way that makes us adults feel like we will be stuck asking the way to the station when we actually want the beach, for the rest of our days. From about the age of 10 onwards kids finally begin to lose this ability, just in time for most of them to begin being taught French at secondary school.

Excellent.

Leaving this educational anomaly aside, it's obvious that very early experiences play an enormous role in how well a child will not only speak, but read and write in their native language. Research has found that parents who spoke to their infants regularly enabled their little ones to learn almost 300 more words by the time they were two than children who were rarely spoken to.[13]

Other studies have also found that just being exposed to language by, let's say, listening to the television (more of which later) adds very little indeed. What children need it seems, is direct interaction with real, proper, actually standing-there-in–front-of-them human beings.

Which begs two questions – how should I speak to my baby and how the hell can I find the time to do it more when I am at work all day?

First, the 'to baby talk or not to baby talk' debate is an interesting one. You may have already come across the school of thought that subscribes to the 'talk to them like an infant and they will always talk like an infant'.

It's normally trotted out by quite annoying people for some reason.

Likewise you may also have been witness to the other extreme – a language so gooey, so dripping with squeaks, raspberries and truncated words that you worry if the deliverer isn't having some sort of breakdown.

The best practice it seems, as is so often the case, lies somewhere in the middle of the two with something called infant directed speech (IDS).

Acting like a Victorian workhouse owner and talking to an 18 month-old-like she's a fully grown adult isn't conducive to optimal language learning for the same reasons thrashing your youngster 23-nil at garden football probably won't plant within them the seeds of a lifelong love of the beautiful game.

Infants need to be given a chance to differentiate between the words they are hearing, so using a more melodic tone with shorter, simpler phrasing gives them that chance.

Using IDS means using many of the same words that come up in every day speech but in a slightly more stretched-out way that elongates the pronunciation of vowel sounds. As well as slowing things down, this also has the effect of sounding more emotionally exaggerated, a way which also seems to help the little listeners comprehend the *emotional* intentions of what's being said.

If you are struggling to hear this happy medium approach in your head, a clever experiment may help you nail it.[14]

In 2007 a team of language and psychology experts found that the way we speak to infants using their first language has some striking similarities to the way we speak to people in their second or third language – we slow things down and extend our vowels a bit.

What we don't do is repeatedly say 'nana' instead of banana or 'time for a liddle nappy nap to bye byes land?' instead of 'would you like to have a rest?'

Using a soupçon of baby language and nonsense talk never hurt anyone and if you're anything like me your heart will break just a tiny bit every time your child leaves behind one of her sweet verbal affectations, but it does seem that to help them the most we should leave what we say pretty much the same but adapt how we say it.

The second question of how you make more time to speak to your child is fiendishly complicated on one hand and the picture of simplicity on the other.

The tricky bit goes back to our look at the importance of childcare. Whoever looks after your child while you and/or your partner are at work has a big role to play in this early literacy development. They will more likely than not be spending a very healthy chunk of the week with your little one, which makes it all the more important to try and find someone who shares the approach of you and your partner – which isn't always easy to pull off at all.

What's more straightforward is to make sure you talk directly to your baby whenever you are doing something together. Commentate on the nappy change, point out the trees and flowers in the park, take them through the Indian menu, anything – just talk to them.

It sounds obvious and indeed is, but children who receive thoughtful, responsive care and attention from their parents and other carers in the first years of life get a serious head start – and we aren't just talking academically here, their emotional well-being has as much to gain too.

When researchers[15] examined the life histories of children who have succeeded against the odds – their surroundings stacked against them achieving – they consistently found a common thread throughout most of the stories; they each had at least one supportive, rock-solid relationship with an adult in their lives that began in the very early years.

Which means it's equally as obvious to state that children who don't often get spoken to or indeed are denied the regular opportunity to explore and play won't just get bored, they will run a serious risk of feeling the ramifications of that rather lonely start in life for an awfully long time.

So we know that talking to our babies and toddlers is a very good idea indeed, all that remains to do now is work out how's best to play with them and which toys will not only keep them amused, but help them develop too.

Simple?

No, not really.

Words from your fellow fathers

Paul, father of two: *I think that the oldest children in a family get spoken to in baby talk and then as people have more kids and less time they ditch it and just talk to them normally which is part of the reason why youngest children are often so advanced.*
Well that's my theory anyway.

Stuart, father of two: *Apart from the 'mama', 'papa' type words one of the earliest ones that stuck in my mind was during a walk in the park and my daughter shouted out 'ree roll' – which after a while I understood as squirrel.*

Nick, father of two: *'mama' was our son's first word but he went on to the use the word 'fuck' instead of 'help'. A lot of problems with that, especially when you consider how many times they ask for help or when they become more independent and let you know they don't want it.*

Toys and the importance of play

You and your partner aren't the only ones who work every day in your house. There is another determined, conscientious and driven individual who puts the hours in at the coal face, come rain or shine.

Play is your baby's work. Yes it's fun, but in terms of development, when the toys come out your child couldn't be doing more of a job if she demanded a one-to-one, told you she was feeling undervalued and threw the odd sickie.

Through play, babies and toddlers explore, innovate, experiment and create – whether it's rolling a car back and forth or looking through an old kitchen roll tube, they will be learning multiple new skills and honing old ones at every turn.

What's more, you and your partner hold the truly great honour of being their first and absolute favourite playmates – a position that in a decade or so's time you will no doubt be clinging onto as they grow closer to their friends and viewing you as a cardigan-wearing fuddy-duddy.

But for now and a good while longer you are the coolest person to muck about with ever – so how do you make the most of it?

Taking it nice and slowly is a pretty good place to start. Show them how to get started but resist the temptation to do it for them while simultaneously helping them enough to keep frustration at bay.

Their's, not yours, I mean.

Then there's repetition.

Then there's repetition.

You will need to get used to doing things over and over again, clapping and cheering with renewed vigour every single time an action is repeated because what you are witnessing is your baby practising and repractising her new-found talents and absolutely loving her own work – and if that's not worth a round of applause, I don't know what is.

As your child grows, her play will become more complex and what she learns from it will become equally as impressive – she will pretend, role-playing herself to a standstill in the process; she will recreate scenes from your very house, mortifying you as she tells off her teddy in the exact same way you have chided her.

Striking the right balance between interacting with and guiding them and just letting them get on with the serious business of playing is important – as is resisting the temptation to see play as somehow a waste of time compared to 'structured learning'.

Playing is learning.

All of which feeds into a much wider debate that will come to impact you in a few years' time – do British children stop playing and start school too early?

A lot of the evidence says they do.

Finnish pupils, for instance start formal education at seven, enjoy mammoth summer holidays and end up with the highest educational standards on the continent.

In the UK our children are among a handful of European kids who start formal school at five and also have some of the shortest holidays to be found anywhere – and yet we languish in mid-table when it comes to the achievement rankings.

What's more, introduced in 1870, this early start had very little to do with educational benefits in the first place according to the Cambridge Primary Review report[16] but rather it was seen as a way of actively reducing the time children spent with their feckless parents.

That wasn't even the half of it. A secondary reason was to keep nervous employers happy – an early start meant an early leaving age and more young workers for the sweatshops.

Makes you proud to be British, doesn't it?

As I clamber down off my soapbox let's focus on how you can help your baby and toddler play, what toys are best and which ones are just enormous pieces of garish plastic tat that will not only survive longer on this earth than our entire species, but will spend most of that time in your loft or garage.

Toys

The international toy market is worth around £50 billion every single year. That's a lot of Sticklebricks by anyone's standards – especially given the old cliché that children are more likely to play with the box than what's in it.

As we've seen, the modern parent has realised that these toys aren't just handy ways of keeping the kids quiet, they are essential tools in the physical, emotional and social development of their children.

And don't the marketeers know it.

There are still toys out there that are focussed solely on fun, but more and more toy brands are tapping into the growing awareness that every second of play is a learning process.

One of the most globally predominant of these brands, Baby Einstein, has been at the centre of a heated legal and media battle over what it claims, or is seen to claim, its huge range of toys can help achieve.

It's incredibly easy to get sucked into this world of guilt purchasing, the guilt deriving from the fact that you are somehow denying your pride and joy a vital and irreplaceable developmental boost by not buying the fully interactive ergonomically centred sensory suite with free 'plot your child's manual dexterity' wallchart.

There's no doubting that some new toys are nothing short of brilliant, but don't beat yourself up if you can't afford to buy them all. A well-thought out, well-researched single purchase is often greeted with much more enthusiasm and engagement than a wheelbarrow full of swag. Present occasions are also the perfect time for your child to receive that fun, educational toy from grandpa or aunty. You will probably shy away from second hand toys first-off – namely because you'll be given many as gifts, but also to put your mind at rest hygiene-wise. However, there's nothing wrong with a well-loved, very well-washed toy!

As a rough rule of thumb from birth to six months toys that stimulate sensory and motor development are the best bet – that's rattles and the like in English. Up to the 18-month mark experimenting and achieving goals is what your child loves to do so the building block, jack-in-the-box toys hit the mark, as do very simple musical instruments.

As they head towards their second birthday, children often engage in make believe and problem-solving play and can match objects by shape and colour. Their vocabulary tends to explode into a riot of new words – so your house will be awash with costumes, puppets, dolls, toddler trucks and bikes.

The third year is when your little genius really starts to hone and master the skills they have been practicing, so you move into the arts and crafts phase. Simple board games may make an appearance and if you've not already been drawn into the world of cars, trains and dolls' houses you probably will be now – not to mention toy cookers, vacuum cleaners and washing machines as your little one wants to act as grown-up as they feel.

So as you can see, you'll get through a few toys! Some items remain firm favourites throughout, some never capture the imagination, others benefit from a spell in the loft and reappear triumphantly like returning gladiators.

Whatever the particular toy box ups and downs in your house, it's wise to take advantage of charity shops, eBay and local second-hand sales if you want to avoid having to sell your actual kitchen appliances to afford the pretend ones.

There's one toy that I've deliberately passed over so far, because despite being simple, relatively inexpensive and as old as the hills, it deserves to be looked at in isolation, such an all-round star is it.

I give you, the humble book.

Books

We already know that early language and literacy development starts in the first three years of life, but what is perhaps more surprising in some senses is just how closely linked that progress is to the child's earliest experiences with books.

Way before actual reading is on the agenda, babies and toddlers soak up literacy learning by the mere physical interactions they have with books, paper and crayons.

Before school appears on the horizon, children are learning to talk, read, and even write by using books and other literacy materials such as magazines and newspapers. They essentially enter the world of words from the very start of their lives and the more they encounter the tools of reading and writing, the more they learn.

In her book *Much More Than The ABCs* Judith Shickedanz[17] outlines categories that can be used to understand the book behaviours of very young children. These categories help us as parents to recognise what's happening in front of our tired little eyes.

Shickedanz highlights the fact that even something as seemingly innocent and simple as your baby handling a book is increasingly being seen as a key building block for adult literacy. Turning the pages, chewing the corners, even throwing books around is all grist to a very important mill.

As your tot grows, how they pay attention to the actual content also becomes key. From gazing at the pictures, chuckling at a favourite page and then pointing to characters or feeling different textures in some of the excellent touchy-feely baby books around, it all represents the next stage.

While this kind of activity has always taken place, what's new is the importance that is being attributed to it.

So, just to recap, watching TV doesn't help children read; has a detrimental effect on their ability to focus and makes them fat.

The reasons TV is suspected of having such a seemingly catastrophic impact on our young are manifold – first, time spent watching TV means less time doing other more productive things, like creative and imaginative play and physical activity. TV is essentially a one-way street flooding information towards the sofa, and not generating much else. When a child is watching TV they aren't socialising or receiving the vital feedback to their actions and behaviour they need to grow and develop.

When you put exposure to advertising into the mix, things get worse still. As well as encouraging demand for material possessions, it's also been linked to the rise in obesity, thanks not only to the sedentary nature of the viewer but also the exposure to junk food that some adverts bring.

The UK's National Literacy Trust, which among other things campaigns to raise awareness of how to regulate a toddler's viewing habits, suggests that rather than switching on the box, parents should:

> *'Limit exposure and encourage other one-to-one language-enhancing activities that centre on talk at mealtime, bathtime, shared reading and imaginative play.'*

So then, to the recycling plant we go, TV sets strapped down to our roof racks like the peddlers of evil they are. The trouble is that television is as much a part of our culture as the motor car we'd use to drive them to their deaths and we all know what a world-ending thug that four-wheeled hunk of metal is.

It takes a family of extraordinary fortitude to completely banish the telly from their lives – and while these families do exist, they represent a tiny percentage of the parental herd of which we are a part.

So what do we do?

The obvious answer is to take a keen interest in exactly what and how much programming our children imbibe, rather than constantly using TV as a cheap childcare option, guaranteed to keep the kids glued to the sofa when we need time to clean up, or try one final time to find the house keys.

While highlighting the negative impact of television on children, the National Literacy Trust are smart enough to recognise that a blanket ban just isn't going to happen and so their advice is to:

> *'Encourage exposure to some high-quality, age-appropriate educational television for children aged two to five.'*

The quality of the output really does matter it seems. Dorothy Singer, co-director of Yale University's Family Television Research and Consultation Center, states that:

> *'Children who are watching good programs do make gains, both cognitively and socially.'*

What constitutes a 'good' programme is down to your judgement as parents. As are decisions later down the line as to whether a TV in the bedroom is a good idea for your children.

But what about computers in the bedroom when your kid's older? What about iPhones in the back of the car right now; what about computer games for infants?

Oh God, why is everything so bloody complicated?

The rise of the i-baby

I remember as a cocky primary school pupil telling one particularly exasperated teacher who was trying to get me to practise and re-practise my absolutely woeful handwriting that it wouldn't matter anyway because I'd be typing everything when I was a grown-up.

What an annoying little bugger.

I wasn't far off, mind you, and as for our children, who knows what the world will look like by the time they are adults, given how quickly things have changed in just the last five years?

But what's the deal with computers and smartphones and iPads? It wasn't that long ago that playing computer games was seen as classic couch potato activity. But now it's accessible everywhere and anywhere, should we now be encouraging our infants to soak up as much new technology as they can, as early as they can, or put this area in the box marked 'when you get older'?

Not only is that a complicated question, it's one that has parents, academics, and medical experts floundering to keep up, not only with the expansion of new technology, its benefits and drawbacks, but also with the rate at which children are becoming exposed to it environmentally.

One of the few bodies looking into this area is The Joan Ganz Cooney Center, named after the driving force behind *Sesame Street*. A report from the organisation called *Always Connected: The new digital media habits of young children*[21] focusses on the rare studies that do exist about young children and digital media – as opposed to the hundreds on how teenagers interact with it and it makes for interesting reading.

It seems that even in America, which as ever (or maybe that should be for now) is at the vanguard of this phenomenon, there are few hard and fast conclusions, let alone guidelines, being drawn up on what's best to do. Instead there is debate – and much of it.

To put it very simply, in one corner you have the increasingly sedentary lives of the children who are exposed to digital media and the negative physical and psychological impacts they can have on them.

In the other, you have emerging evidence that 'well-deployed' digital media can generate fresh skills, higher levels of achievement and allow children from different backgrounds, creeds and even continents to make connections in ways never before dreamed about.

As you may have guessed, what 'well-deployed' actually means is pretty much down to you as a parent. With almost all the research available focussing on children of eight years or above, your guess really is as good as anyone's on whether letting your two-year-old play around on your iPad is a good thing or not.

While the report makes the oft-stated point that platforms and outlets themselves aren't the issue and the actual content they are exposed to is where the hub of the 'digital media good or bad for kids' debate sits, it also concludes that what research there is provides strong evidence that the media habits of children are seriously out of whack.

It recommends that:

> *'We need higher-quality educational offerings to promote*
> *critical thinking for children and adults in their*
> *selection and use of media. While we can imagine a*
> *day when young children themselves will produce their*
> *own media, for the time being they are still counting*
> *on us!'*

Then there is the rampant commercialism at play. In their book *Consumer Kids*,[22] Ed Mayo and Agnes Nairn paint a picture that makes televisual advertising targeted at children seem positively benign.

They argue that while parents seem to have registered the threat of sexual predators who make use of the power of the digital space, they have no clue how their children are groomed for profit. They say:

> *'The screen can no longer be classed as an electronic*
> *babysitter that keeps children occupied. It is a whole*
> *electronic world in which they are immersed and which is*
> *underpinned firmly and securely by a profit motive. It's*
> *the commercial world that dominates the time of today's*
> *children.'*

Right, that's it, never mind the telly, every digital device in the house is going in the bin first thing in the morning.

Be still my beating reactionary heart – the truth is, it's just too early in the game to make those kind of calls. Although there's precious little research out there to tell us if the other side of the coin actually exists, there is one report, carried out by the same people who drew together the *Always Connected* paper mentioned earlier.

Learning – is there an app for that?[23] looks at what it calls the 'pass-back effect', a term which beautifully captures the moment you may well soon recognise – if you don't already – when you pass your mobile device, children's app already loaded up, to the back of the car.

Shameful – but according to the report it's a rapidly expanding phenomenon, so you are in good company.

The report found that – surprise, surprise – even very, very young children picked up the skills needed to use these devices at an almost indecent speed – especially when it comes to the mega-intuitive, touch screen kings like the iPhone.

And do they actually learn and develop by using these apps? The report, albeit slightly hesitatingly says yes, early evidence suggests so and what's more it goes on to recommend that American educationalists should 'optimise children's time with mobile devices' and even 'use mobile devices as supplemental tools.'

But what about you and me? What does it say our role should be in this new era of the pass-back? Well apart from the almost obligatory statement that it's basically all down to us to regulate and balance exposure to mobile devices and specifically the content on them, it goes on to add that:

> 'When it comes to smart mobile devices, many parents do not yet view them as potential learning tools – and thus restrict how their children use them.'

Which sounds a lot like 'get with it, Granddad' to me.

So all in all it's safe to say that the jury isn't just out on this whole digital/kids debate, the courtroom hasn't even been built yet. As with television exposure, keeping a very close eye on the amount and quality of your child's interaction with digital media feels like the smartest route we can take in lieu of any cast-iron evidence either way.

One thing is for sure though; if you've ever seen the way a toddler grasps touch screen technology within seconds, you'll know it's built with them in mind much more than us.

....

Words from your fellow fathers

Winston, father of two: *Television is a necessary evil where parenting is concerned. There is a lot of interesting stuff on the BBC too and Mr Tumble is a genuine star, of course.*

Tom, father of two: Pingu *should be part of everyone's life. Question is how much and what constitutes too much TV.*

   It's always when you've had a 'DIY' weekend where you've used TV to occupy them a little more than you should have, you feel guilty and then the first thing you read in the Metro *is yet another bloody UN report on how bad TV is for kids!*

   The spectre of advertising to kids is only just coming into effect as we're moving away from the mothership of CBeebies to the commercial channels.

   It completely sucks, there is so much of it and the kids seem to treat them like programmes. I would love it to be banned.

Chris, father of two: *All advertising annoys me and having worked in the media I am very sceptical of it. I hope to instil that scepticism – or at least questioning nature – in my kids when it comes to ads.*

Paul, father of two: *I'm constantly torn between thinking that allowing my youngsters to play on the iPad is a good or a bad thing. Instinctively it feels lazy and a waste of time they could be spending running round outside. A nagging voice in my head tells me that this is the kind of technology (and way beyond) that they are going to live their entire lives with and they should get on board as early as possible.*

The deciding factor is often that it keeps them incredibly quiet and entertained!

Your progress report

Your baby

So what else are these cute little learning machines up to during these few months then?

A lot.

They could well be drinking from a cup like a seasoned pro by now and a fork and spoon could be a big part of the meal time routines too. Still lots of food on the floor and walls, but there will be an increasing panache to the way they catapult that ravioli square gracefully through the air.

New words appear at a dazzling rate now too – go out in the rain and the chances are they will come out saying a baby version of umbrella and melting your soggy heart.

Walking increasingly becomes more doddle than toddle as they gain confidence with every step, amazing you and your partner as they stop, bend, pick something up and move on – a skill you would probably struggle to replicate given how knackered you are and how creaky your back is.

Don't worry if it feels on occasion like the progression you expect is interrupted with your little one becoming scared of things that they used to take in their stride, like the vacuum cleaner or even the bath. Much the same as with separation anxiety, this is progression, as their senses unfurl and their independence grows they will take against things hither and tither just because they bloody well can.

You'll probably find yourself saying 'Where's your nose? Where's your nose?' and other body part location-finding questions a lot now, too, as they revel in their ability to find them. The more fuss you make when they point to the right area, the more they will want to do it and the more you will fall in love with them.

Glory days, soak up every second you can.

Your partner

If your partner's back at work, the childcare carousel will be in full spin. As we've touched on, when childcare is good, it's a relief. When, for whatever reason, it's a cause for anxiety it can consume every waking parental moment. If that's the case for you, the chances are you can multiply the worries you have by a factor of 10 when it comes to your partner.

There's little more unsettling and upsetting for a mother than having to leave their baby somewhere they are less than 100% happy about. Perfection, as we all know, is pretty thin on the ground in any walk of life, so try your best to be alive to any childcare worries your partner may be having.

If you have the beginnings of a fussy eater on your hands, this too can be a huge angst generator. We will look at this in detail a bit further down the track but it's worth remembering that where toddlers are concerned tomorrow is most definitely another day. What gets hurled on the floor one day may be ravenously devoured by the end of the week. Help your partner not to overly fret as your little one is sure to pick up on her stress and dig her heels in even more. Keep persevering with different foods.

You

How are you, love?

No really, how are you?

Worried about work, about the mortgage, about not being at home enough, of supporting your frazzled partner in the way you'd like to? Or just loving every single second of being a dad so far?

The answer is you're probably all of those things before you've managed to put on your socks of a morning.

We can be awfully tough on ourselves and each other as new parents and the truth is we are learning constantly. When and if number two comes along, a whole new set of challenges and questions arrives too and I've a feeling they just keep on coming in different guises for good now.

Having someone you love and care for more than anything else in the world changes you for good and almost always for the better in every direction – so give yourself a break and enjoy it.

As we've been talking about all things technological the digital world has made it shockingly easy to bring work home nowadays too.

You know what I'm talking about – the winking BlackBerry on the side, pulling you in like a siren – MUST CHECK EMAILS –

or the laptop begging to be opened, whimpering in the corner, a Pandora's box enticing you to release its treasures.

Burying the BlackBerry in the sock drawer of an evening or leaving the laptop at work sounds easy and for some it probably is, but talking to lots of new dads, struggling to keep their jobs secure in the middle of tough financial times, it's a real issue to switch off.

I'd love to be able to help you out but as a major culprit myself I'm in need of assistance, too. What I do know is that in years to come, the chances of me remembering that staggeringly annoying email I just had to respond to at 7.15 on a Tuesday evening is minuscule compared to the time my son finally caught his first ball and ran round the garden like an Ashes winner.

MONTHS 17-20

Getting away from it all

As you begin to really settle in to your new life as a father and at least a semblance of normality returns to your life – or a new version of normality – you might just find yourself contemplating all sorts of things that just 12 months ago seemed unthinkable.

We're not necessarily talking about that John O'Groats to Land's End bike ride you've always half fancied in a not very serious sort of way, and that extension to the kitchen can wait a little while longer too, but it feels like your robust, inquisitive little youngster is ready for a holiday.

Lord knows, you and your partner could do with some sun on your backs and a little reward for the stunning child-rearing job you have been doing thus far too – so that's it settled then – we're all going on a family holiday.

As with much – well everything really – in your life now, your considerations when deciding where to go and how to get there have changed somewhat. So in this chapter we'll take a guided tour through the whys, wherefores and WTFs of getting away from it all with a wee one in tow.

Hopefully unrelated to your travels, (but often not) your toddler's ever-growing pioneer spirit not only keeps you on your toes and helps her learn and develop in all sorts of ways, it occasionally results in her putting herself in harm's way – which often leaves you and your partner as the first line of medical support.

Unless you're a doctor, nurse or health professional yourself (in which case you couldn't have a quick look at my ankle could you?) the chances are your first aid skills amount to a dog-eared card in your wallet which proudly states that you undertook basic training in 1998.

Now is a very good time to brush up, and we'll look at some of the most common things you could be called on to deal with.

Not that you should live in a constant state of bowel-opening worry of some hideous fate befalling the most precious thing in your world. But let's be honest, even the most confident and gung-ho among us occasionally succumb to a phenomenon that seems to have arrived in spades at roughly the same time as your child did – fear.

Where your children are concerned, love and fear are two sides of the same coin, increasingly so in a world where we are constantly reminded of the threats and risks that seemingly lurk like smirking traffic wardens around every corner.

How do you keep fear in check while the love you feel climbs ever skyward as your relationship with your child grows by the day?

In short I don't know, and I don't think anyone else does either, but let's delve into the issue and see if we can't make ourselves feel a bit better about it, shall we?

Have child, will travel

You've seen off the tough early days; family bliss has broken out all around and you fancy a break, no not a break, what you fancy is a family holiday – the very words turning you into your parents the instant they pop into your head.

Getting away from work, away from the house, away from those black bits that seem to be coming off the bath mat – all these things are good.

God knows your partner would appreciate a change of scenery, having you around 24/7 to share the load, you might even be able to reacquaint yourselves with one another as the holiday spirit takes hold and the day to day duties of parenthood take a back seat for a while.

Your adventurous little one would love it too, new terrain to cover, new faces to frown and then smile at, new cupboards to open.

Let's go.

The only tiny thing is, parenthood doesn't stop just because you are on your holidays and that new terrain your baby will relish needs to be chosen with care. These aren't big issues, though. We can do this, all it takes is a bit of planning.

Where to go
Home

Babies and toddlers get to every corner of our green and pleasant land on their jollies nowadays it seems.

Such is the scramble to get hold of parental disposable income 'family-friendly' is replacing 'no football coaches' as the sign you are most likely to see on your holidays in the UK. Stacks of highchairs can be found in restaurants far and wide and soft play areas now live where the pool table used to in lots of pubs.

Holidaying in the UK with your kids has never been more popular, primarily it has to be said, because of the economic climate rather than a positive change in the meteorological one.

But there's no doubt holidaying in the UK has improved as an experience since our day. Facilities are better; there's more to do when the heavens open and businesses of all hues are practically yanking you and your buggy off the street to relieve you of your spending money.

Yes the weather has gone nuts, lurching from sun that we can't deal with to rain fall that flash floods the bejesus out of us before lunch time, but you can't have it all, can you? You know the lingo, you know the food and you know the water's safe to drink – and for many parents embarking on their first holiday is all that counts.

Then there's the fact that your little one can do the whole thing in the comfort of her own car seat. Of course six hours to Cornwall is a bit different to a jaunt to Sainsbury's so more food, more liquid, more wipes, more everything is needed, including – as you'll find as you are forced to weld the boot shut – more car.

What's really essential is a flexible attitude. A seemingly enormous six hour on the road allocation might seem generous, extravagant even, before you set off, but a baby crying in the back of the car isn't only tough on the eardrums, it is also dripping with so much argument producing venom that it beggars belief.

Add in a spot of map reading and the baby monitor beeping in the boot like R2D2 on smack and you've got yourself a holiday hydrogen bomb. Best to take it nice and slow, plan some stop-offs on the way to really stagger the journey or even stay really local to up the holiday and cut the travel time.

Away

Transferring an infant to extremely remote, exotic or warm destinations takes either a lot of bottle or a complete lack of marbles.

The obvious health risks that apply to you when you spend two weeks somewhere unfamiliar are magnified many times for your baby. Extremes of temperature, ropey sanitation and just general culture shock can turn your holiday into a nightmare for all concerned and a jet-lagged toddler is a sight to behold I'm sure.

Sunburn early in life for instance is more likely to cause skin cancer later on, so a constant round of factor 50 application, shade hunting and hat replacing will be called for if you chose somewhere that's baking.

People do it though, for some it's to see family, for others a statement of intent that their pre-family wanderlust shall remain. Eyes wide open and meticulous planning is the way to go if you take it on.

For most, though, a trip abroad with a small child means Europe or at a push the US. Thousands upon thousands of families head for Spain, Portugal, France, Italy and, increasingly it seems, Turkey every year. Many of these destinations enjoy a well-earned reputation for being brilliantly child-friendly, the locals whipping your children from your arms to coo over them in a way that would have you screaming the place down back home.

A small tip – if you are planning to travel within the EU get hold of a European Health Insurance Card (EHIC) for every member of your family It will make accessing health care, should you need it, a million times more straightforward. You can find them on the NHS website.

Ferries full of top-box carrying cars make the journey to mainland Europe every summer, others take the Channel Tunnel and yet more take to the air.

Children on aeroplanes – now there's a thorny little issue. Cast your mind back, if you will, to your pre fatherhood days. You take to your seat, glance left and see an already rampant toddler yanking at the hair of the woman in front, as the mortified parents apologise at the rate of a sorry every nine seconds while still managing to fit in the time to tear strips out of each other about who forgot to pack the raisins.

Let's hope for your sake that you showed these poor people kindness – because if you didn't the forces of kiddiewinkle karma will in all probability smite you down with such vengeance that you'll wish you had opted for two weeks under your kitchen table.

Small babies can be a doddle on flights – they just sleep, eat, smile, sleep. It's when they start to move and wriggle and attempt to open the doors that the fun really starts. But hey, it's only a few hours isn't it and if people imagined there'd be no children on a holiday flight they'd obviously started on the Ouzo before they left.

Hand luggage crammed full of nice food, copious drinks and as many books and toys as you can jimmy in will serve you well. Producing a never before seen item can also be a boon and as we've already discussed they bloody love your mobile phone, don't they.

Where to stay

Where's best to lay your hat for a fortnight with a little one in tow?

Hotels are an obvious option. Many offer kids' clubs that you can take advantage of during the day if you are so inclined, so for a few hours at least you and your partner can really unwind and talk to each other about something other than percentile points, teething gel and why your bubba isn't clapping hands, pointing and playing the tambourine like the high achiever from the NCT group.

You'll probably end up talking about all that anyway, but you'll just be able to do it while reclining on a sun lounger with a cheeky cocktail in your hand.

Where hotels can start to lose their lustre somewhat is in the evening. Unless you are comfortable taking advantage of any babysitting facility that's on offer you'll probably end up staying in your room – which is great if you are flush enough to book a suite, or even somewhere with a decent balcony. If you can't, you might find yourself playing cards by head torch in a pitch black room and trying to eat crisps in silence.

Funny and sweet and romantic for about 25 seconds then actually quite rubbish.

Also don't worry if you start to wonder if the travel cot will fit in the bathroom, you're not evil, we've all had those thoughts and some of us have even carried them through.

Then you need a wee at midnight.

Hiring your own pad is another route – whether that be a cottage, villa or apartment.

The benefits here are obvious, you have more than one bedroom – unless you have booked spectacularly badly – and a kitchen to cook for yourselves and baby.

Asking for high chairs and travel cots to be provided is a good idea as is requesting a stairgate. What a website will describe as child-friendly can often be anything but when you arrive. And for the love of God don't rely on the photos, they lie. Childproofing an entire holiday cottage isn't on so you might need to be canny about where the baby zones are and shut off the jagged, super slippy marble staircase with a strategically placed armchair.

Whatever bricks and mortar accommodation route you go for, one thing you must never, ever, forget to take with you is some sort of light black out material or blind. Many a curtain rail has been yanked from its moorings by desperate dads as they perch on a chair and attempt to attach a three-tonne blanket to the window using stolen pegs, some plasters and a size 4 nappy.

Which leaves us with the king of family holiday environments, a double-edged world where when it's good it's very good, but when it's bad it's wetter – camping.

Many people can't abide the very idea and would rather spend a week on hold to BT.

For others, the pull of the open air and the whistle of a camp stove kettle is irresistible, and campsites, especially in the UK have never been better equipped or more numerous.

Likewise for tents, the new-fangled materials they use to make them mean they rarely let in water and no longer require a doctorate in engineering to put them up – a mere diploma will suffice nowadays.

Get the right weather and your toddler will be in heaven, roaming around without a care in the world and taking in so much fresh air that bedtime is embraced like an old friend.

Then it's onto the deckchairs and hello to the sauvignon blanc.

Get the wrong weather and you are just a tent peg or two away from hell. Monopoly and Bop-It might keep older kids happy, but a wet toddler, in a wet field, with wet parents is hard for even the most annoyingly enthusiastic among us to pull from the doldrums.

If you get lucky you'll have a ball and you'll wish you'd have invited your friends and family – or maybe you did?

Who to go with

You're a ready-made family unit now so why on earth would you need anyone else on your holidays?

Well, not to beat around the bush, there's babysitting. Taking Nana and Granddad doesn't just mean they get to spend some quality time with the apple of their eye, but you just might get some time alone, too.

As for holidaying with friends I'm sure there are parents out there who have been away with pals who don't themselves have small children, but I'd put a small wager on them never having done it twice. Feeling guilty about broken nights, heinously early mornings and the inability to indulge in the vacation antics of the childless must weigh heavy on that kind of arrangement.

Or maybe that's just me being too much of a weak-willed wuss, maybe these people need to know the reality of the parental situation, maybe they need to see for themselves the hard work that parents put in, maybe they need to do alternate mornings.

Maybe not.

There is another option, that you get together with people in the same boat as you. You can all do the mornings, share the bathtimes, keep an eye on each other's nippers, who in turn have a playmate – and the grown-ups might even have a night out each.

What's not to love about that?

In my experience very little, sharing the load and a few laughs with parents of children around the same age as yours can be a great way to do things. Yet there's seems to have been an awful lot written recently about the pitfalls of such arrangements, especially when it comes to taking infants it seems.

First of all you've got the fact that people have the habit of going away with a couple they only know because they happen to have a baby the same age and have perhaps only met in an NCT-type environment. I can see how this could unravel in quite spectacular fashion

A spot of lunch in the local pub surrounded by a wagon train of buggies is very different to a fortnight getting to know someone else's parenting foibles. It may seem perfectly natural to you that your child needs to fall asleep to the digitally remastered version of *Stairway to Heaven* every single night – to your vacation companions this may, alas, appear a little strange and even, whisper it, annoying in the extreme.

Perhaps worst of all though, so the horror story articles go, you've got the exposure to other people's relationships as seen through the parental prism. What if the other father doesn't pull his weight in anywhere near the same way that you do? What if he is an unreconstructed non-dad who barely notices his child, let alone the mountain of jobs that need doing to keep it alive on a daily basis?

Awkward!

I say awkward when what I really mean is 'get in'. You will be in so much clover as you feed, bath, entertain and soothe your toddler, while simultaneously administering an Olympic standard foot massage to the mother of your child, that you could rip your flight ticket asunder and float home.

But what if, pity me no, but what if you are put in the shade by your opposite number? What if your fatherly efforts, hitherto in your mind's eye worthy of some sort of humanitarian award, are eclipsed by the picture of paternal perfection you have foolishly chosen to entrap yourself with?

That's never going to happen, is it – you are untouchable, hear me, untouchable.

Pick the right people, don't be afraid to go off and do your own thing and you'll be fine, honest. Who knows you might end up with holiday buddies for life which will mean one thing for sure, the kids will always have a ball.

Don't panic: first aid for parents

It's no coincidence that we turn to first aid straight after family holidays. The change of terrain and climate has a nasty habit of throwing up a minor emergency or two.

In reality, it's your home where the danger lurks and it's a good idea to be prepared.

Baby first aid courses exist and are worth doing, but if something happens to a newborn you hit the phones to medical experts pretty quick.

It's when toddlerdom starts to beckon that a whole host of relatively minor injuries and conditions can and do crop up that are still quite painful for them and frightening for you.

Trained medical help should still be your default setting if you at all worried or feel out of your depth. When my younger boy recently beat the unbeatable child lock on a kitchen cupboard and mistook a Fairy Liquitab for a bright blue marshmallow he did what any of us would do in that situation and took a lovely big bite out of it.

DON'T PANIC! I just about managed to blurt out through the blind panic I was feeling.

A call to the much-maligned NHS Direct saw me transferred straight to a nurse and then speedily onwards to the National Poisons Information Service (who knew we had one?) who looked up what a liquitab lunch would do to an 18-month old and gave me the appropriate advice, all within 10 minutes of the call being put in.

You can't knock it, no matter how much we all do.

Aside from instances like that when nothing but expert help will do, there are a whole host of situations where knowing some good basic first aid procedures will serve you and your new family very well indeed – here are some of the more common ones.

Cuts, scrapes, bumps and bruises

As well as the really minor and incredibly frequent knocks that your toddler will pick up you may well need to give some TLC for slightly more hefty knocks.

Knowing when expert help is needed is half the battle in the first place. The advice is that if the injury is less than half an inch around, there's little or no bleeding and once the initial shock had died down they don't seem to be in excessive pain, you can deal with it yourself.

Other than that – and especially if it's a bump to the head or if you're just not sure – get it checked out.

If it's a cut, it's worth remembering that things almost always seem worse than they are when blood is around, so keep calm, take a good look at the wound with clean hands before deciding if you can deal with it.

If you think you have it covered, rinse the area by holding it under the tap and dab it dry with a sterile swab if you have one (a decent first aid kit is a purchase worth making, for sure).

Then you can put on a spot of antiseptic cream if you like and finally pop on a Mr Bump plaster. It doesn't have to be Mr Bump but his backstory can help to make your injured little soldier feel in good company.

If there's bruising, you can try applying a cold compress to reduce the pain and swelling. Bruises are blood clots and the worse a bruise looks the more it's clotting and healing.

That's right, your mother wasn't lying to you.

If the bruising is really severe, covers a large area and doesn't show signs of getting better after a day or so, it's another trip to the GP surgery for you. If only they gave Nectar points.

You can try arnica to reduce the swelling too, if you fancy. As with almost all homeopathic remedies, some people swear by it while others swear at the very mention of it.

Choking and swallowing things they shouldn't

My God, it's scary when a child chokes on something. In fact they don't even have to choke, just a splutter while finishing off an apple juice will have parents lurching towards their offspring in full 'ready to react' mode.

If something serious happens on the choking front, it's really worth knowing your first aid onions because time is very much of the essence. No one wants to think they might be put in a position where they have to save their child's life, but it happens every day.

Now I could try to explain the dislodging and resuscitation procedures here, or you could even buy a specialist first aid book. But by far your best option is to book yourself on a toddler cardiopulmonary resuscitation (CPR) course pronto (the NCT run a good one) and get some hands-on practice at what you need to do.

It's incredibly easy to mean to do something like that and forget, but it's a skill you may need in a very big way one day soon, so it's worth making the time and doing it.

As you'll no doubt know by now, babies and toddlers learn about the world around them by touch and taste and if it fits in the mouth it will jolly well go in the mouth.

It's for this reason that more than 500 under-fives are rushed to casualty each week in the UK because it's thought they may have been accidently poisoned.

Yikes.

Medicines are the most common culprit, with everyday painkillers top of the list, presumably because we parents are much more lax in terms of locking them away safely. That, and the fact that we always have a bloody headache.

Although more and more detergent nasties are being made with bittering agents that make them taste so immediately foul that kids spit them straight out, it's far from being a universal practice – so the obvious safely precautions need to be taken to keep dangerous items well out of reach at all times.

Including liquitabs.

Heat stroke and dehydration

Heat stroke is a life-threatening condition and children are especially prone to it

It occurs when the body's temperature rises while its ability to cool off shuts down, and nippers don't need to be in tropical climes to get it. Playing outside in hot weather coupled with not getting enough liquid down them can be all it takes. It can also happen if they are overdressed or left in a parked car where temperatures can rise much higher than those outside.

Your toddler may well first show signs of heat exhaustion, like thirst, fatigue, leg or stomach cramps, and cool, claggy skin.

If not addressed, they may then develop any of the following symptoms: hot, red and dry skin, a rapid pulse, confusion, dizziness, headache, vomiting and eventually unconsciousness.

It's not pretty, this.

Dehydration also has tell-tale signs, such as your child going six to eight hours without a wet nappy, lethargy or even a lack of tears when crying, which sounds so tragic it's almost beyond belief. If dehydration worsens, you could see much worse, such as sunken eyes.

If you even half suspect heat stroke you need to first call 999 and then bring your toddler's internal temperature down as quickly as possible before they slip into unconsciousness. You can do this by undressing her completely and laying her down in a cool area. While the ambulance is on its way sponge down the body with a sponge dipped in cool water and fan her, too.

With dehydration it's best not to faff about, either. If you suspect it's reached serious levels make the call as your child may need to be given fluids intravenously. While you are waiting, try and get an electrolyte drink like Dioralyte down them.

Burns

Burns! Man alive, we're getting heavy now aren't we?

Well yes and no.

We're not necessarily talking house fires here – hot drinks are the number one cause of scalds amongst the under-fives. A youngster's skin can be anything up to 15 times thinner than an adult's and hundreds of children are admitted to hospital with burns or scalds every week.

For less serious burns you should cool the area by submerging it in cold water rather than under a running tap, which can be too abrasive. Leave it there for at least five minutes, preferably 10. Then gently dry the area with a clean towel and cover it with a sterile bandage.

Much like bruising, blisters are a good sign that the healing process is under way, so don't pop them, just add a little antiseptic cream and cover the area loosely with a clean non-stick bandage.

Even if the burn itself doesn't seem too serious, if it's larger than two inches across or on your child's face, hands, or genitals, or if it has been caused in any way by electricity or chemicals, seek medical help immediately.

Aside from those exceptions, mild first-degree burns like this may well heal in a few days, but anything more serious needs immediate medical attention too. Don't attempt to treat a more serious burn yourself, just place a clean sterile cloth over the area to keep germs out while the medics arrive.

Whatever the cause, whatever the damage, witnessing an injury to your child will shake you to the core. Try to keep a cool head and resist the urge to shriek like a banshee. You will be of more use to your poorly child, who is so attuned to your behaviour and feelings. So count to 10, man up and do it for the kids; if you panic and appear anxious they can easily become even more distressed.

As well as how you react during and after an event like this, an interesting thing tends to happen to a lot of men when they become dads – the love they feel for their children, combined with the primeval duty they feel to keep them safe, come together to create fatherhood fear – and lots of it.

....

Words from your fellow fathers

Marcus, father of four: *With the second and third ones casualty was like our second home.*

We are still in the habit of arriving anywhere (on holiday, family visits, etc.) and checking out where the nearest casualty department is before we do anything else. We have visited casualties in Spain, France, Italy, USA, Germany, in fact every country we have ever been to. And babyproofing has never been any help.

Colin, father of two: *Our daughter broke her leg when she was 18 months. . .it was awful. She stepped off the bottom step of the stairs (4 inches) and twisted her ankle. It was missed by the X-ray and wasn't diagnosed until two days later. . .rubbish time.*

Nick, father of two: *A few falling off beds, etc., but no great dramas with the first one. My second couldn't spend enough time in casualty – or so it seemed. It looked like her every action was designed to get her there as quickly as possible.*

Ben, father of two: *Our son fell off the changing table, while under the control of my wife. We rushed him off to casualty and he was given the once over and was fine.*

My wife has never forgiven herself, mainly because the doctor was a stunning young blonde who laughed at all my rubbish new dad jokes.

Needless to say I got up that night to do the late feed.

Love and fear

The love

It's often said that fathers truly fall in love with their children a bit later down the line than mothers.

The theory goes that newborns only really have eyes for their mums and the bond between the two is often so instant and strong that as men we only really get the chance to feel the full force of parental love when our little ones begin to show their personality and engage more with the world around them.

There's also the claim that babies tend to be born looking more like their fathers than they do their mothers to give us an instant and needed physical sign that the little person who has just been born really is our progeny – evolution's very own instant paternity test.

A couple of studies even back this hypothesis up[24] with test groups having significantly more success matching photos of babies and their fathers together than with shots of the mothers.

Whether or not there's any truth in both of these thoughts, once the love drug properly kicks in for you, whenever it happens, you'll certainly know about it because there's nothing else quite like it.

Even the most narcissistic, self-absorbed and selfish among our number tend to be gripped eventually by a feeling so deep in the chest, so adept at flooding our systems with potent hormonal narcotics that it can stop our egos dead in their tracks.

The first time you see your toddler's innocent interest and friendly advances towards a slightly older child spurned, you will almost certainly feel like someone has yanked your heart from its protective rib cage, placed the still-beating lump of muscle in a blender and made a smoothie out of it.

How could that big brute dismiss my sweet, well-meaning naïve little one like that? You'll want to scoop her up and smother her in a blanket of affection and love, hoping that the cruelty of the outside world is kept at bay for a little while longer at least.

In a year or two's time it will be your baby that's dishing out the brush-offs to the younger set as they get in the way of the stairs to the slide – but that doesn't figure right now – what gets you is the rejection they've

175

suffered, even though they know very little about it and continue to totter around in blissful innocence.

It's getting me going and I wasn't even there.

That's just one of a million instances that can and will make you realise that you don't control the love for your child, it controls you. Just wait until your son or daughter comes home from nursery with a bite mark on their arm. Plans for fiendish and satanic revenge attacks will pop into your mind and you'll temporarily shock yourself with just how emotional you become.

Most of us manage to tame these reactions though, thank goodness, and sure as eggs is eggs, the bitee has a good chance of becoming the biter at some later stage.

The strength of your feelings doesn't just demonstrate itself when injustice and retribution rear their ugly heads. The overwhelming pride we feel as parents at the progress our offspring make also has the power to leave us acting in a very different way from our pre-parenthood days.

Even if you are acutely aware of the pitfalls of becoming a baby bore, even if you have almost melted with embarrassment and annoyance in the face of a father telling you in great detail that their cherub not only eats broccoli by the field load, she does so mostly with a knife and fork and on the odd occasion chopsticks – you, too, will fall foul.

It's impossible not to at some point – even if it's just to yourself in the mirror – and there's nothing wrong with it. The ultimate paradox of parenthood is that on a macro level 250 babies are born every single minute of every single day somewhere on the planet – it's nothing special, in fact in many ways it's perhaps one of the most inevitable and everyday things we ever do as animals, next to sneezing and eating too much cheese.

Yet on the micro level it dwarfs all the other things we treat as important to us, it makes us think, act and feel differently and often with more intensity than anything else we ever experience – it makes us *really love*.

So if you feel like telling the world how bloody great your child is, you go right ahead. Just don't overdo it, all right? The rest of us have just eaten and besides we know for a fact that it's our own babies that are the real stars of the show.

So we've established that, as Wet Wet Wet suggested, love is indeed all around when you become a dad, but it's not alone. It has a shadowy, unpredictable but no less powerful brother: fear.

The Fear

It stands to reason, really.

When you love something so very much you also become apprehensive, worried, even paranoid about bad stuff happening to it.

On its most basic level there are physical threats, such as cars.

If I think too long about roads and traffic and parcel delivery vans driving down residential streets as if they are planning to take off at the end of them, I get an urge to weld my jack-in-the-box son's bedroom door shut.

I will only release him, I think to myself, when he has demonstrated to me by way of a series of independently verified examinations and vivas that he has developed the wherewithal to convince me that he is among the safest and most conscientious pedestrians in the country.

How he will gain this knowledge confined to his bedroom I'm unclear on, but it is a trifling problem compared to the dire alternative.

The fact that the UK has one of the best road safety records in the world is immaterial to me when I am in this state; it appears to my fearful mind as positive propaganda pumped out by the evil cartels of motor manufacturers, tarmac layers and bone idle lollipop operatives hoping for an afternoon or two off work.

It's easy to get carried away when the fear grips you see.

Then there's stranger danger.

On average 11 children are killed by a stranger each year (compared to 124 child road deaths in 2008) and statistically children are at a much higher risk of abuse from someone they know. Yet despite the stats, the news coverage that these utterly tragic stranger abductions and deaths create, precisely because they are so unusual, instils what looks on paper like a disproportionate level of fear in parents.

Our fear glands aren't made of paper, and the sheer horror of contemplating even for a nanosecond that something like that could happen to your child has curbed the freedom we afford our kids, especially where outdoor play is concerned.

This fear-driven change is increasingly seen by some as playing its part in the increase in social disorders and behavioural difficulties that is being seen in the country's children.

A combination of fear of the bogeyman and the risk assessment culture that we increasingly live in is increasingly cutting back on the opportunity our children have of developing in the time-honoured way of learning from their mistakes.

As Sue Palmer, author of *Toxic Childhood* puts it:

> '*All real children's play involves an element of risk, and the more real play children are allowed the better they become at analysing and managing those risks.*
>
> *If, on the other hand, adults try to eliminate risk from their lives they're likely to grow up either unduly reckless or hopelessly timid.*'[25]

And so it is that just as love generates fear, so fear begets guilt, guilt that you are being over-protective, or too reckless, or, as we shall discuss later, focussing too much on the need to be the provider that you spend all your time working and not enough playing.

It's a decidedly complex balance to strike for the modern parent and it's made even harder by the fact that as a couple you and your partner must work to find a common approach to fear and risk with which to bring your children up.

You may be petrified of the roads; she may be more concerned with the effect TV adverts are having on your little one. You might think your toddler should be allowed to climb to the top of the big slide; your partner may think you have lost control of your senses.

Having the courage to overcome your fears and anxieties and let your cherished child explore and learn, while keeping them safe and secure, is truly one of the most important and difficult of all the skills you need to perfect as a modern parent.

The nature and form of the way you set boundaries and instil discipline soon enters into the equation too – but that is another issue for another chapter. For now, as you begin to refine and redefine your approach to loving them so much on one side of your brain and being petrified of something happening to them on the other, rest assured that every other parent on the planet is wrestling with the same dilemma as well.

Know too that it will never, ever end.

Once your fear of parked cars has eased it will be replaced instantaneously with anxiety about exams, then alcohol, then killer drugs masquerading as plant food, then your child's job security and enormous mortgage and then, well then it will begin all over again when you wonder if your grandchildren are being kept inside too much.

Yes indeed, the love and the fear is part of the long-term parenting package and as you will have no doubt found already it isn't just mums who worry, not by a long chalk.

Words from your fellow fathers

Winston, father of two: *You become more fearful of accidents when you become a parent, not just to your kids but to yourself and your partner too.*

Chris, father of two: *I'm not an anxious person and I always believe things will work out, so I don't have that over-riding fear that I see in a lot of parents. In fact I believe that fear is a negative thing that is harmful to children. I worry like any parent about them being good people, being nice people, and enjoying life. . .I guess I just have to show them that life can be joyful, that anything is possible and I realise the rest is up to them.*

I think the only thing that really scares me is the harm the world can bring unexpectedly – but if I teach my girls NOT to get in a car with a young drunk male, then things will be OK. I know that my kids need to know risk, they need to be in risky situations, and hopefully I can equip them with the notions of how best to deal with those situations.

And in a way I think (minor) bad things happening is part of life and that's how we grow. So if they don't make friends instantly at playschool, that's fine. . .that's life. . .I am confident that my kids will be able to move on and deal with it.

Paul, father of two: *The more you grow to love them the more you worry about them. As I'm dropping off to sleep I'll sometimes replay stuff that has happened during the day and start to play out all of the 'what ifs' – what if I'd not got him before he climbed the stairs, what if she'd have pulled the kettle off the work top.*

If I go too far my eyes open automatically as if my brain is saying, 'stop this you fool'. It's a powerful thing indeed.

Your progress report

Your baby

We're about halfway on the road to your nipper celebrating her third birthday – but as we stand here proudly at the midpoint, jam on our shirt, two giant Duplo blocks in our work bag and the whereabouts of the back door key still unknown, we can see that our 18-month-old is much more of a toddler than she is a baby.

Yes indeed, she has come a long way from the startled little extra-terrestrial we brought home from the hospital. For starters she has a grasp on the language which could at this stage even constitute combining two or even three of her newly learnt words together to form rudimentary but surprisingly efficient sentences –'more grape Daddy' certainly does the job for instance. By 20 months, she could even be stringing two sentences together.

You might also notice that she's beginning to recognise that some things are different and some the same, you might stumble across – or more likely into – a pile of toys clumped cleverly into groups of all the same colour or shape.

This may not be the most spectacular development you'll witness but when you think how important the basic skill of being able to differentiate is to us you can see why it's a milestone in its own right.

Living in Britain as we do it's important to us as parents to instil into our children the custom of saying 'please' at least three times when requesting something and firing at least five 'thank-yous' out on receipt of said item. As for 'sorry', well you just can't say too many of those can you – preferably before, during and after an event that almost certainly wasn't your doing anyway.

Well, the good news is that your child can now begin the process of being inducted into our politeness club and by far the best way to make that happen is by being polite when you ask her to do something.

Your partner

Whether your partner is at home, at work or a mixture of both she will be putting in what contemporary football managers seem to refer to as a 'shift'.

Or put another way, working her arse off.

Toddlers are demanding little beasts both physically and mentally. They are sometimes still seriously attached to their mums and often don't like it when mum dares to go somewhere else and increasingly have the tools to let her know their displeasure in the most vocal way possible.

We'll be looking at tantrums, discipline and all things terrible two in the next chapter but for now be aware that toddler wrangling is tough work and your partner needs all the support she can get from you – especially if she's trying to juggle a job and worrying about childcare at the same time.

There's a chance that rather than having a toddler of the clingy and screamy variety, you have a super independent little person on your hands – which is great, but can leave some mums wondering where their little baby has gone all of a sudden. This in turn can trigger thoughts and conversations about doubling the number of children in your house.

More of which later.

Finally, take a good look at your partner the next time you get the chance. She has carried, delivered, nurtured and loved your child these past 29 months or so and if she's anything like most other mums on the planet, she'll have done it all brilliantly. It's astonishing to behold but tragically easy to miss in the heat of the family furnace just what a formidable feat this is.

It's the size of the achievement that can also sometimes see new mothers at this stage struggle to remember who they were before they became an expert on the merits of Bugaboos over Maclarens.

So enveloping is early motherhood that recalling that other things, other people and other places once existed or even just vaguely remembering that the sofa wasn't just for wiping clean, but actually sitting on, isn't a given by any means.

Letting her know what a great job she's doing, what a great mother she has become and that over these next 18 months you'll do everything you can to help her experience a life outside motherhood, would be a very nice thing to do indeed.

You

Been to the gym lately? Or for a run?

Thought not.

Finding the time to exercise as a new dad – and mum for that matter – can be a nightmare. Spending all day at work means you want to get home PDQ to see your family before the small one goes to bed and the bigger one dreams of doing the same.

Taking the time to exercise in this world can feel like the height of self-indulgence – 'shan't be home for bathtime tonight, off for a workout, sauna and long hot shower' *isn't* a note you want to leave on the kitchen table.

The paradox is that if ever there was a time in your life that you needed the manifold mental and physical boosts that a spot of regular exercise can bring, it's now.

So what to do?

Better to try and squeeze the time from your employers than from your family, so is a lunchtime run a possibility, or a bike ride to work? If not then at the weekend why not turn the lunchtime nap into a proper walk for you and your partner. Not a stroll round the block, a long pacey walk for a good hour or so that can blow the cobwebs away and get your endorphins flowing.

Although it might feel like the very last thing you feel like doing you know deep, deep down in your weary mind that you'll feel better for it.

What's more the post-bathtime beer or glass of wine that has become like an old trusty friend to you these past months will taste all the sweeter knowing you have at burnt at least 8% of its calorific value off earlier that day.

Whoop!

Months 21-24

The twos: just how terrible are they?

As you approach the completion of your second year as a father there's much to be proud of.

Your walking, talking little wonder is a credit to you and your partner – you've nurtured, loved and guided her to this point and as you sit and watch her play, a warm feeling of pride and contentment will no doubt wash over you.

And then, from nowhere, your cherub will take a cup from a shelf you didn't think they could reach and throw it with unerring accuracy and admirable power into the very heart of your flat screen TV.

Yes that most hackneyed of all child related phrases the 'terrible twos' will soon start to be uttered to you knowingly by those further down the parental line as you attempt to cope with a tantrum so explosive, so volcanic, that Sky News are running it as a breaking story.

Meltdowns, biting, hitting, pushing all of these things will need dealing with to varying degrees. In this chapter we will delve into the world of discipline and look at the different approaches and techniques employed so you can choose the one that fits you, your partner and your toddler.

Wrapped up in the discipline debate can often be the 'wait till your father gets home' syndrome that exacerbates the situation in which many men find themselves. Thanks to the enormous amount of time they have to spend at work, they come a distinct and distant second to Mummy in the affection stakes.

If this applies to you, you'll know that the grown-up thing to do is shrug it off, trot out the line about it being a phase and generally man up. But we both know that when it happens it hurts, so seeing as we are among friends, let's see what can be done.

At this stage of your nipper's life there are also often some big girl/boy moves to be made too – firstly there's the shift from the cot to the bed and then, if you employed it in your battle against sleep deprivation months back, there's ditching the dummy.

As if that wasn't enough at this two-year mark, there also used to be an across the board health visitor check-up to gauge your little one's growth and development, but in many areas that seems to be going the way of libraries and pot hole filler – into the bin marked 'austerity measure'.

It's still worth going through your own checklist at this point so you can proactively raise any worries you might have with a health professional, even if they no longer have the resources to make it their business to give your toddler the once over themselves.

Discipline: surviving the terrible twos and beyond

Discipline.

It's an ugly word isn't it, dripping with undertones of the cane, the headmaster's office or the Sergeant Major's growl.

Not a word we should be letting within a mile of our beautiful little bubbas, with their smiles, their innocence, and their sweet naïveté.

The thing is, though, all the developmental milestones we cheer at, all the new skills we proudly tell everyone we know about in minute detail, all of these things represent another step towards your child becoming independent, becoming a person.

And we all know what people are like. They have an annoying habit of seeing things in their own way, of making choices we wouldn't, of loving what we loathe and loathing what we love.

So as your baby grows – even in their first year of life – they begin to understand that they have the power to make decisions, to register displeasure, to disregard advice and to do what they bloody well want.

It just so happens that for many youngsters this realisation first dawns at around the end of their second year, hence the terrible twos. Your child isn't being terrible though, she's just doing what you would do if you thought you could get away with it, if you hadn't been socially conditioned and handed the fig leaf of embarrassment to hold.

With younger siblings this 'spirited' enlightenment often kicks in earlier thanks to the role model they have who sussed out that 'no' was a small but powerful word many moons ago.

Don't misunderstand me, I'm not non-conformist or stupid enough to be suggesting that the world would be a better place if we ditched discipline and let the children run free to grow up without boundaries.

That world would need to be transformed into a vast soft play area to cope with the fighting and biting we'd all indulge in when some other bugger has stolen 'MY' parking space.

But seeing it in these terms helped my tiny brain to stop chucking out empty phrases like 'why can't you just listen?' and 'I've already told you' when all the irate toddler before me was really doing was flexing their new found 'me, me, me' muscles.

You need a bit more than just an holistic outlook to help you cope with a supermarket tantrum or a bite mark so deep in the flesh of a fellow nursery goer that you wonder if there's not a big cat living under the sand pit.

There are techniques and tips to help you and your partner dispense discipline when you see fit, but understanding what's behind it is a big help. As well as just the natural exuberance that boundary pushing creates, there could be a whole host of other factors at play, too.

Young children are remarkably sensitive to change, for instance, be that moving house, an alteration in their daily routine or losing attention to a sibling – and this unsettling change can often lead to testing behaviour.

Then there are the old familiar factors that used to generate a cry in the early months – tiredness, hunger, boredom, frustration – but which now produce so much more colourful a reaction. I mean, why merely cry when you can throw a fully loaded yoghurt pot at a fully loaded clothes horse?

Then there's personality and character. Are you a bit of a one? Do you throw the odd wobbler? Well, chances are your little mirror image might have a dash of that fighting spirit in them too – which you'll admire and despair of in equal measure.

Whatever the underlying reasons, there will be times from this point onwards when you will need to get across the message to your toddler that painting cats is never OK – or that taking from them the lethal glass photo frame they are holding is actually an act of love, rather than the act of war their resulting meltdown seems to suggest they regard it as.

Tactics and techniques

Before we look at ways that you can communicate with and calm a toddler who is in full furious flow it's interesting to look at why and when your child's behaviour presses your buttons.

Some things are a no-brainer; anything that is potentially harmful to them or others lands right on your fear gland and triggers an immediate response.

But what about the more borderline stuff – do other factors affect when and how you respond?

Most of us, it seems, tend to chide our children more when we are in front of others – especially other parents or our own parents – than when we are alone at home. It somehow feels a very British thing to do, not just because our child's behaviour could directly affect the people we are with, but because our parental credentials somehow feel under scrutiny, because we and our offspring could be judged and marked down as bad eggs.

It takes courage to go against the wisdom of the group and either refuse to pick your child up on what others see as beyond the pale, or reprimand them for something you see as wholly unacceptable, despite it being the norm for the rest.

That interesting little phenomenon aside, here are a few of the key areas to think about when you begin to try and tame your toddler.

Make sure it feels right and that you are both water tight.

The absolutely key thing is not only to do what feels right for your child, but also to form as super strong an alliance with your partner as you possibly can. A child, even a very young one, can identify a wafer thin fissure in your approach to discipline from 30 paces and in time they will turn it into a yawning great chasm between the two of you – which isn't good for anyone.

Talk with your partner and try and find a way you both believe in. Honesty is key too. If you are trying to live by a set of rules or a philosophy that you don't believe in, children, like dogs smelling fear, will spot you a mile off. If you don't mean what you are saying, don't say it.

Be persistent and consistent

Disciplining your children is a pain in the arse, pure and simple.

It's much easier to let it be and ignore it, than it is to stick to a route, saying the same lines over and over and over again – but that's exactly what you have to do.

This stuff takes time – even the fabled 'naughty step', now the discipline destination of choice for millions of parents thanks to Supernanny Jo Frost, is far from a quick fix. No, it takes dedication, determination and patience to follow your plan through, whatever it may be.

Also, with childcare playing an increasingly large role in our lives as parents it's also worth speaking to whoever looks after your child to make sure you are all at least reading the same book, if not on exactly the same page of it.

Avoid over-reaction, encourage conversation

Easier said than done, this. When your child does something irritating for the 23rd time that hour even the more saintly among us is tempted to press the nuclear button. Likewise when they do something that puts them in serious harm's way and shocks the living daylights out of you it takes real resolve not to let your feelings flood out.

I'm useless when it comes to this last one – especially where roads and cars are concerned as I perhaps gave away a smidgen when we discussed fear. All of my well-thought-through discipline techniques momentarily go out of the window such is the liquid anxiety coursing through my veins, when there is even a hint of traffic danger.

Do my histrionics freeze my son's feet to the pavement? Yes! Do they teach him the Green Cross Code? No.

Talking to our children to explain why we don't want them to do a particular thing is a far more preferable and profitable route to go, as is encouraging them to explain their frustrations or thoughts. Even at this age it's worth doing; more will stick in both directions than you think.

Again in my case that reasonable approach escapes me momentarily after what I perceive to be a near-miss because at that precise moment I seem to be watching a disaster movie in my head which has my little one as the main character.

Don't forget the good times

When you are going through a difficult spell with your child and you and your partner begin to have coded 'We Need To Talk About Kevin' conversations it's incredibly easy to overlook all the good positive little things that are happening before your eyes.

If anything the praise volume needs to be turned right up during a tough behavioural time, not down. Letting them know that a lot of what they do makes you happy and crucially gets your attention will encourage them to do more of it.

If the only time they seem to get attention is when they draw a 15ft purple line on your kitchen wall you could soon have a matching one in every room.

Rewards

What's the difference between a reward and a bribe? The academic answer to that question lies in the presence of prior knowledge.

The practical parenting answer is based more around who cares.

Rewarding people for good behaviour works. We all know that to be true, that's why we turn up for work each morning and praise our boss for their foresight, vision and gravitas.

Remember to be specific if you use rewards. Just handing out Percy Pigs without linking them to a very recent action will leave you with an empty bag and very little else.

Be warned though, you have a finite amount of rewards at your disposal before you reach what is known as 'peak reward' – the point where the amount of times per day that your child think they deserve a reward totals more than the amount of Percy Pigs in the supply chain.

This is a dark place to find yourself and as we will see, with potty training potentially around the corner you may want to keep some of your reward powder dry to help you out.

Distraction

Look, there's a fox in the garden!

Those seven words served my sister remarkably well throughout the bringing up of her four daughters. All of the girls turned out exceptionally well and only two of them have a thing about foxes.

Distraction is the thinking parent's way to avoid or curtail a tantrum. On its own it doesn't teach them the difference between right or wrong, or that roads are dangerous (have I mentioned how dangerous they are?) but it's a very useful thing to have in your tantrum tool kit.

As your kids get older, the equivalent of the fox line will need some creative work doing to it – look, there are two foxes in the garden – that kind of thing, but the chances are distraction will become like an old friend by the time you are the age where you are the one who can't remember what you went upstairs to do.

The Voice and The Look

Everyone raises their voice to their children at some point or another – everyone.

Even the couple you know who seem to have the patience of Job and the resourcefulness of Mary Poppins will lose it once in a while and give it some verbal revs to get their point across.

But while everyone does it no one really likes doing it, or enjoys it – I mean what kind of beast would you need to be to take real enjoyment from rendering your children petrified by bellowing at them?

Nevertheless, shouting is a dirty little secret we all occasionally share, but what can we do to minimise it?

Meet tone. Tone is shouting's smarter, less socially awkward and better looking little brother. If you can master the use of the tone of your voice as a register of either your displeasure or alarm at your little one's antics you can save shouting for those rare moments when absolutely nothing else will do.

Then, if you are really talented and you can combine tone with The Look – well you are almost home and hosed. An infrequently used, well-delivered and unmistakable look can be a very powerful thing and has the capacity to silently communicate all you need to get across without making everyone else in the room know about it.

It takes practice to perfect The Look, so you'll need to spend some time in front of the mirror until you can really get through to yourself.

Mind your language

I don't mean swearing, swearing is fine, swear away. Kids never ever repeat your profanities, especially not out loud in the middle of nursery, or in front of the doctor and they absolutely never say 'Fuck It' when they drop something while being looked after by your mother.

Never.

No, what I mean is that the language you use plays a key part.

First, there's overuse. If you repeatedly use the threat of a consequence to stop your toddler doing something, you will have to either be prepared to carry that threat out at some point or take the phrase out of circulation once it's become redundant.

And it will become redundant sooner than you think, because you will use it hundreds of times more frequently than you realise.

'If you don't behave we will go home right now,' I say for the 14th time that week.

'No we won't' – thinks the bright little person before me, 'Not once have those words ever been followed by an immediate return to our house. Besides, I didn't ask to come to this supermarket/wedding/job interview, you brought me here. I'd quite like to go home actually, there are toys there and what's more when we are at home you at least stop threatening me with immediate return to the bloody place.'

Then there's the altogether more murky issue of the actual words you use. In 2006 Annette Mountford, chief executive of the parenting organisation Family Links, ran into a storm of political-correctness-gone-mad flak when she suggested that calling children 'naughty' damages their self-confidence. She also suggested the naughty step should be renamed to avoid children thinking it meant they themselves were naughty.[26]

She also made the point that saying 'what you did was naughty' rather than 'you are naughty' sent out a very different message.

Mmmm. Tricky one.

Whatever your take on this, an interesting exercise is to replace the word naughty with stupid. Children do naughty things and children do stupid things, but actively telling them that they are stupid feels wrong on a lot of levels. If you've ever heard a stressed and harassed parent do just that, or if you've been that parent, you'll know that it just intrinsically feels like a very bad thing to do.

A smart technique that a lot of nurseries seem to use is not to tell the children what they are or how they should be feeling after they have done something obviously wrong, but rather to let them know that their actions have made the teacher feel 'sad'.

Yes there's an element of emotional blackmail in that, but for my money given how important it is for children to feel like they are gaining praise and acceptance, that is a powerful method of registering displeasure which avoids the need to repeatedly tell the child that they are in some way substandard or different.

If that's a controversial issue, this final one is the daddy, mummy and primary caregiver of all discipline debating points.

To smack or not to smack?

First things first: so far I'm not a smacker, or a slapper for that matter, if you see what I mean – and while we're at it to my mind the only use a cane should have in a school is to grow tomatoes up.

But, a) my eldest child is only four as I write this so there's a whole world of trying of patience still to come my way which could turn me into a serial thwacker and b) what the bloody hell do I know anyway?

Having established that, let's look at where we stand legally and socially when it comes to smacking.

The law currently states that parents can smack their children, but it is illegal for them to leave any mark or bruise. The smacking of children in schools, both state and private is illegal, although nannies and babysitters can be given permission by parents to administer 'reasonable chastisement'.

A 2006 survey found that seven out of 10 parents smack their children and what's more would strongly resist any move to ban corporal punishment in the home.[27] This is juxtaposed by pressure from leading children's charities and the European Union for an all-out ban – a situation that exists in many other countries.

So in essence it seems we have a situation similar to that surrounding the death penalty in that most people when asked want it, but dissimilar in that, for now at least, that popular support hasn't been disregarded by our lawmakers.

Putting aside these parts of the debate though, does smacking actually work to instil discipline? Well, on one level we all know it does – smack a child hard on their bare legs and they won't only stop what they are doing, they will remember the pain and try and avoid feeling it again.

But what about the long-term effects and consequences? Does the often repeated paradox of punishing a child for hitting someone by hitting them really present a long-term problem or is it just a line trotted out by wet liberals?

Well let's just say it's a confused picture.

On the one hand we have surveys which seem to show that children spanked frequently at age three are much more likely to be aggressive by the time they are five.[28] And others that even suggest that children who are smacked end up with a lower IQ.[29]

Then we have research which finds that youngsters smacked up to the age of six do better at school, are keener to attend university and even do more voluntary work![30]

Just to confuse things further, the very same paper also found that if you continue to smack children after they are six it has significant negative effects.

There's also the survey of parents themselves which found that four out of five think smacking is neither useful nor effective.[31]

All clear? Good.

The truth is, no one knows – and ultimately for as long as some form of corporal punishment is available to parents it is up to their gut instincts as to whether they resort to it.

One thing is for sure though: if you and your partner hold concrete but differing views around the smacking debate you need to talk and iron them out pronto, having the conversation after corporal punishment has already been meted out will make a tough issue even harder to resolve.

Up until now we've focussed on your reaction to your child's behaviour rather than the behaviour itself. That is primarily because young children can find so many ways to test you that it's hardly worth beginning to list them.

But there is one area that worth touching on because not only do most of us have to deal with it as parents in some shape or form, but it also happens to be uniquely disconcerting when our angelic tot begins to indulge in it.

Hitting, biting, pushing and kicking

Most young children occasionally bite, hit or push another child – although hopefully not at the same time.

Many even go through spells where they regularly dispense violent retribution like a vigilante cop operating on the margins of the law. While these periods are generally and thankfully short lived, they can seem to go on for eons, such is the perturbation they cause the mortified parents.

I remember my son pushing a fellow toddler clean off a stage area at a christening once. Such was the force of the shove that the boy seemed to travel a good six feet laterally before gravity was even aware of what was going on and intervened to bring him back to earth with a painful-looking bump.

'Oh my God, we've spawned a monster' I remember thinking as I took him outside for a talking-to. What could he be thinking; did he not know that kind of behaviour could seriously hurt someone?

In a word, no, he didn't know that. In fact he also didn't know what would happen if he pushed someone off a raised surface. So he tried it and as experiments go it garnered pleasing and relatively spectacular results.

Until told otherwise, everything is play to young children, including what happens when you sink teeth into a fleshy arm. This behaviour doesn't mean they will grow up to be aggressive but it is your job to get the message through to them that this particular set of games is not good.

From the strictly logical perspective, the most straightforward way to demonstrate just how much a bite hurts is to have a nibble on your child. This is a very bad idea on a number of levels, not least of which is the fact that biting kids will see you in prison – even if your defence consists of 'I was only showing them how painful it is m'lud'.

In fact in 2008 a mother was jailed for five months for doing just that.[32]

So with that 'see how you like it' route out of the question, what can you do to make sure they know that this is serious stuff?

In terms of immediate action, you can tell them in a calm but stern manner that what they have just done is not acceptable. As long as you are absolutely prepared to carry it out at the very hint of a repeat offence you can tell your child you will take them home or up to their room if they do it again.

If they have indulged in a real spate of pushing and biting type behaviour rather than the odd one-off incident getting to the bottom of the root cause is the key. Are they feeling insecure about a new baby, or frustrated by recent change? If you can identify and address what's worrying them, you can often stem the flow of what's driving them to lash out at source.

Talking to them about how they are feeling has the added benefit of adding emotional language to their ever-growing vocabulary – which means eventually when they feel frustrated they may well tell you so rather than launching the next toddler that walks past them into space.

....

Words from your fellow fathers

Jason, father of two: *I am definitely the bad cop, not intentionally I just follow how I was brought up.*

Oldest one is a Mummy's boy for sure, although number two seems to smile at me more so far.

There are naughty corners, steps and zones everywhere in our house and he is happy with them all. He would probably be happy in a dungeon. He does not understand the concept of punishment, or do we not know how to dish it out?

Rob, father of two: *Pure mental toughness is needed to avoid a meltdown.*

Try not to raise your voice at all. Kids at this stage tend to copy exactly what you do. Firm language without any stressful tones is the best way in my eyes.

Mark, father of one: *You have to back up each other whether right or wrong (you can have those discussions afterwards on your own) as you can't have the little one playing you off against each other.*

I'd also pick your battles, no point saying 'no' or being harsh if you don't really have to be. But when you mean it, follow through with it – or you're in trouble next time!

I always tend to kneel down to their height but can't help myself shouting sometimes.

Tom, father of two: *The worst tantrum I've witnessed involved noises that I can only describe as beyond feral. Generally over something so trivial.*

You find yourself sometimes coming up with ridiculous threats like 'if you don't behave, Christmas will be cancelled'. I did pretend to call Father Christmas once, and he was mortified – my son, not Santa.

Felt a little harsh but once you start, you've got to see it through of course, otherwise they realise you're crap at making up threats. Very clever, are children.

Simon, father of one: *My son is very easily distracted away from tantrums it seems. Especially by chocolate of any description.*

Marcus, father of four: *Our second was a biter. Would rather my child was bitten than was a biter, it's very hard to deal with.*

Stuart, father of two: *Our eldest was very much a biter (as was I as a child – drawing blood after biting my uncle's bottom after an excitable game of 'horse').*

On a few occasions she would latch onto my cheek with her teeth while I was play fighting with her. Her younger sister is a pusher, which she finds hilarious.

I want Mummy to do it: second-best syndrome

Life isn't fair – we all know that. It has the distinct habit of wedging the gusset of justice up the backside of hard luck and delivering something we didn't expect or deserve.

And so, brave father, it is my duty to tell you that although you may well have done everything that could have been reasonably asked or expected of you up to this point and then some – your child probably still favours their Mummy and may even tell you so on a frequent and not so sensitive a basis.

That's OK, though, isn't it? Mummies are soft, mummies understand and well, everyone loves their mum. And besides, we're grown men aren't we – it doesn't bother us one bit does it?

In public no, in private, well maybe a little.

The odd 'I want Mummy to take me to bed' we can all handle – but if there's a noticeable and persistent desire to be with mum rather than dad it can really hurt, despite our male programming telling us to suck it up and make like it doesn't matter.

There could be two main factors responsible for these instances of mummy favouritism. The first is if you have already found yourself acting as the primary disciplinarian of the family. Playing the 'wait till your father gets home' role can be an effective deterrent for misbehaviour, but it can have the very real side effect of positioning you as the villain of the piece.

While being bad cop doesn't really mean much with a two-year-old, fast forward 18 months and you could find yourself in a place you neither expected nor enjoy. The temptation then is to redress the balance by sanctioning all sorts of stuff you wouldn't normally and generally acting the goat – all of which can lead to 'silly Daddy' syndrome.

Without wanting to disappear into the debate about the role men now often play in modern society, you can see plenty of 'silly Daddys' in action across a lot of children's TV. It's quite rare to see a father character being portrayed as anything other than either a well-meaning clumsy clot or parental law enforcer. What the sociological reason for this is, is open to debate but the upshot doesn't make for the most rounded viewing.

Back in the real world lurching from good cop to bad cop is a very tricky role to play and if you can, it's much more preferable if you both take a hand in all areas of parenting so your child can form a balanced view of both of you.

Aside from defining your day-to-day role as a father, there's another more influential factor at play when it comes to why many a youngster favours Mummy – the fact that many of us fathers simply find it impossible to spend as much time as we need to with our children.

When you are trying your best to juggle work and home responsibilities, it can be hard to hear from your partner that the reason your child isn't as close to you as you'd like is because you don't spend enough quality time with them.

But it's probably true.

How precisely you are meant to rectify this sad situation is one of the modern father's main conundrums. Torn between a primeval instinct to provide and the desire to interact with our children we spread ourselves pretty thin, truth be told.

Would missing that late meeting really make that much of a difference to your job? It's hard for me to say without meeting your boss – but giving it a miss to play on the carpet with your nipper is definitely worth a go every now and then if you can.

The adage 'things will pass' is also worth remembering if you are getting the cold shoulder from the little person you love most in the world. It may only be a matter of weeks before your child enters a stage where you give her exactly what she wants and needs at that point in her development and then mum is the one with the moist eyes and the hangdog expression.

What's more, as fortunes and affections swing back and forth you and your partner can at least console yourself with the knowledge that in a decade or so's time when you have a teenager on your hands neither of you will be flavour of the month.

Words from your fellow fathers

Winston, father of two: *My little girl used to tell me 'Don't want Daddy' and sometimes even 'Don't like Daddy' when she was around two. It upset me greatly as I would wonder what I had done to deserve it. My wife would dish out fearful bollockings to her for being mean to me, and it is surprising to realise how easily hurt I could be by a small child. I knew it was just a phase and it passed.*

My son who is now nearly two has suddenly become protective of his mum and loves her in a different way from his sister. But he looks at me differently too and, poor boy, you can see a degree of hero worship. He'll grow out of it when he realises his dad's a dufus.

Chris, father of two: *I'd come home from work all geed up to see my daughter, open the door and get blanked. . .it was crushing. I understood it, but was crushing nonetheless. I do tend to be favoured when it comes to wrestle time and 'throw-your-kid-as-high-as-possible-in-the-air' time.*

Oh and 'can I have a lolly' time – I'm a little softer touch there.

Stuart, father of two: *As Mummy was the worker in the family I would routinely be dropped like a bucket of sick as soon as she got in from work and then at weekends Mummy would have a permanent little shadow.*

I do think absence makes the heart grow fonder, though, because when I have freelanced, when I got in from work I would be met with two very excitable children, very happy to see Daddy.

Canning the cot and ditching the dummy

Being two can hardly be classed as over the hill, but the difference between the toddler you know now and the newborn you began your fatherhood journey with is truly astonishing.

Walking, talking, laughing, joking – there's a whole range of complex activities that your little one can do without even thinking about it.

As she continues to learn, she also starts the process of shedding the things she needed to help her on her way from baby to mini person. The move from the cot to the bed is one of those significant little moments.

Even more visible a sign to the outside world that the baby days are being left behind is saying so long to the soother, for those still using them – and with medical advice suggesting that use much after three years old can interfere with tooth alignment, many parents use two as the point at which they try and pull the oral plug.

Moving to the big bed and ditching the dummy can be a natural and smooth progression which your child accepts with the wisdom of someone who's moved on these last 24 months.

Alternatively they can kick off in a big way and bring sleepless nights temporarily back to your world.

You remember those, don't you?

The Big Bed

There's no hard and fast time when a child should move from a cot to a bed – although by the age of three most have jumped ship.

In many ways if she is comfortable and sleeps well in her cot only a fool would move her unnecessarily.

If, though, she is outgrowing their cot, arms and legs sticking out this way and that – or as my son did at just over two, clambering out of the bloody thing in the middle of the night and hopping down the landing in his sleep bag complete with chipped tooth and bumped head – you'll know it's time to make the move.

Another trigger is if there's another baby on the way and the current tenant of the cot needs to make way. If this is your reason, try and ensure that your toddler is well-settled in her new bed before the interloper arrives to avoid fanning the flames of disgruntlement.

Some children will adjust easily to a big bed, they'll love it even, thriving on the grown-upness, the space, the freedom – whereas others may not like it one little bit.

Chances are your firstborn will be the one most likely to kick up a stink because it may be one of a raft of changes to broadside her little life, like going to nursery or expecting a brother or sister. Later-born children also have the benefit of wanting to do exactly what their older siblings do too – and may well see cots as for babies.

If you are sensing unease, little touches like putting the bed in the same place as the cot was and transferring the same blanket across can really help.

As ever, getting them involved in picking the bed and the bedding is also a great idea – foster a sense of ownership of the move in them and you could be on to a winner.

No matter how prepared your child is to move to a bed, though, a guardrail is a must, without a support of some kind they can easily toss, turn, roll over and end up in a heap on the floor. Although you can buy beds with these built in, it's best to buy a separate one so you can take it on your travels with you and make any bed safe.

As for the bed itself, a lot of people go for the cot bed nowadays which via the magic of the Allen key sees a traditional cot transform into a cute little mini bed. The only drawback is that if you have a second child you need the cot back and either have to turf the toddler out (not great for sibling rivalry) or buy a whole new one.

Another possibility is visitations. Once they clock that they can get out of bed, their next move could well be the door and then your bed.

There's no way of combating this other than through patience and firm but gentle encouragement to stay in bed if she wakes up. Often this passes quickly but it can turn into an epidemic, five, six, seven times a night either going in after hearing her walking around or having to carry her back to her bed after she's snuck into yours again.

If this becomes the case, rather than contemplating locking them in, don't be shy of reaching the conclusion that you may have made the switch a touch too early and going back to the cot until they are ready.

Ditching the dummy

I know dummies get a bad press, but for their size and relative cost, they can deliver an extraordinary amount of contentment to small and big people alike.

If you used the little plastic wonder, there's a chance that for certain parts of the day or night it is still working its sleep-inducing magic and if that's the case you and your partner will have almost certainly had fitful conversations about how and when you pull the plug, as it were.

No one really likes how a dummy looks on a two-year-old and if it spends too long in the mouth of an awake child it can and does have a detrimental effect on tooth alignment and even speech development – but the peace and rest it brings is a hard thing to meddle with for all concerned.

But once you finally bite the bullet and decide that the time has come, there are some tried and tested ways to do it that can avoid the kind of bedtime Armageddon that your imagination can dream up.

The technique to avoid is stealthily stealing it and playing dumb as they become grief stricken. Not only isn't that a very nice thing to do, it's not a very clever thing to do either, because the trauma that the sudden and unexplained disappearance can cause them, dwarfs the removal of the thing itself.

No, the collective wisdom of those who have done it says that gradually decreasing the times it's used without so much as mentioning your evil master plan is a sensible start. Once you've got dummy use down to, say, bedtime and the odd cold that crops up, you can move on to the end game.

When the big night arrives it's a good idea to have gotten rid of every dummy you have stashed away in the house and the car, because if things kick off in a big way you'll want temptation well out of your eye line rather than winking at you from the changing table.

A visit from the dummy fairy remains a popular way to soften the blow, with a nice big boy or girl present left behind in its place. Some enlightened dentists – as opposed to the stupendously petrifying ones we used to go to as kids – can now even help you out too and the really cool ones sometimes have a place for youngsters to deposit their dummies in exchange for a sticker or toothbrush.

Times have changed.

Depending on your child, a little explanation and story like that might be all you need to smoothly say 'sayonara' to the soother and gently sneer at those who took great pleasure in telling you that you'd have a nightmare on your hands once they carried on using it past six months old.

Or you might find yourself in a situation where for three or four nights on the trot your house reverberates to the sound of an incandescent and terribly upset toddler. There's no easy fix for that as we all know, but if you see the dummy as having provided them comfort there's an argument to say that for a while you and your partner need to replace what's lost, so it's extra kisses and lashings of warm cuddles all round.

That and bribery, don't forget bribery.

Check me out: your child's health and development at two

There used to be a time when the two-year check-up was a rock solid staple of the parenting calendar.

Most often carried out by health visitors, it took place at a key time of change for the child and acted as an across-the-board check on how the nation's toddlers were getting along and if they were hitting the right milestones at the right time.

That's not the case now, though.

Over recent years budget cuts and shortages in health staff have seen many areas have the two-year check suspended or even abolished, replaced sometimes with a letter sent out to give parents pointers on what to look out for, but often with nothing.

If you happen to be in a part of the country that has kept hold of this important check, chase them up and get an appointment. If not here's what your child would have been checked for.[33]

Gross motor skills

Child can:

> walk and run without falling

> walk upstairs and downstairs holding on and using two feet per step

> throw a ball forward without falling over

> walk into a ball to kick it.

Fine motor skills

Child can:

> build a tower of 5–6 bricks

> imitate a circular scribble and straight line

> turn the single pages of a book.

Vision

Child:

> recognises pictures of animals and everyday objects e.g. cup, apple, banana in picture books

> has no squint.

Communication and hearing

Child can:

> name 3–5 pictures or objects

> use about 50 understandable words and understands more

> make little sentences of two words e.g.'Mummy's keys'

> tell you what she needs

> carry out simple instructions.

Social skills and behaviour

Child:

> plays with toys meaningfully and in make-believe play

> has little idea of sharing but may be beginning to take turns

> plays alongside other children rather than with them

> is very possessive of own toys

> can drink from a cup and feed herself with a spoon

> is very curious and tries to investigate everything

> has no concept of danger

> has temper tantrums when frustrated but easily distracted

> may have toilet awareness e.g. know when wet or soiled.

Before you run screaming to the GP's surgery, as ever it's vital to remember that all children progress at different speeds in different aspects of their development. Some are great talkers and lousy runners and vice versa.

Having said that, these two-year check-ups haven't been scrapped because all of a sudden they have become a bad idea, or because somebody realised that 24 months was actually a rubbish age to take a look at how things were going, they have been cut because of cash – pure and simple.

So, if you are worried about something specific it goes without saying, get it checked out. Eye tests are especially important; one survey found that 34% of parents with school-aged children (five to 16 years) have not had their child's eyes tested in the last five years,[34] despite guidelines suggesting that children be taken for an eye examination by the age of three and every two years after that.

Your progress report

Your baby

As we've seen, your toddler's personality and imagination are growing and developing at a fantastic rate at this age. With that growth comes the likelihood that they will begin to become scared of things.

It could be monsters, strangers, a character in a book they have been reading or the dark.

Listening to these fears, letting them know it's a natural thing to feel and even that you are sometimes scared of things will go a long way to helping them to learn how to deal with a feeling, let's be honest, that will be with them on occasion for the rest of their lives.

When they are brave, tell them how proud you are of them and make sure they know that you will always be there to help make them feel even braver.

On a more physical level your child will start to favour either their right or left hand from this age onward. Up until now they will have been switching from one to another, trying them out essentially.

The whole 'handedness' thing is still a bit of a mystery but what is known is that genetics plays a big part and around one person in 10 is left-handed. You'll soon know if your nipper is part of the lefty crowd.

As for walking – pah! Try climbing or even the odd run for size. She might be trying to kick a ball now too, although not always with the desired result and the comedy routine that is missing the target, spinning round and landing on her bottom can be often enjoyed.

Jumping, which it turns out is anatomically really quite tricky to get to grips with, is still a little way off, though.

Put some music on and you might also be treated to a little dance too – more often than not an impossibly cute bobbing up and down number.

You and your partner

Here's a word you and your partner are about to hear a whole lot more of –

'Why?'

Be careful on that slide.

Why?

Because you might fall off.

Why?

Because it's a long way from the ground.

Why?

Because you need the height differential to be able to slide down it.

Why?

Because if it was flat you'd just lie there.

Why?

Because gravity wouldn't be able to exert itself.

Why?

I don't know, do I look like Isaac Newton? Ask Mummy.

They will want to know everything and in their eyes you know everything. So for the next 19 years don't ever stray too far from Google.

What's also about to appear on your radar again is birthday time!

While the second birthday isn't quite as much as a milestone as the first the good thing is that while you still haven't reached the territory where 30 other parents abandon their children to your care for three hours while they go shopping – your toddler will love a bit of a get-together, even if they might not be fully aware why it's happening.

Your house is still the best venue and any more than 10 kids can not only be hard on the old eardrums, but also quite overwhelming for little ears, too, and any more than a couple of hours is overkill at this age.

You don't have to blow a fortune of fancy stuff and grand themes; it'll still go way over their heads. No, a dressing-up box, plastic party horns, a story or two, a sandwich for them to throw and some cake for them to eat will do the trick and have them begging for more. Or a nap.

If anyone suggests party bags to you, tell them they are definitely on the agenda for next year. Definitely.

YEAR 3

Months 25-30

Fancy another?

All two-year-olds are brilliant.

Yes, they can lose their rag, yes they rapidly begin to think they are invincible, and yes their running about and gung-ho chips are fully functioning while their danger one hasn't kicked in yet.

But they are still brilliant.

They want to know everything, to feel everything and to do everything. In their minds they are the kings and queens of the universe – no one has ever learnt more than they have as quickly as they have.

Imagine feeling like that! No wonder they go berserk when we stop them from opening a mere cupboard.

In keeping with this spirit of derring-do and the transition from baby to barrier-busting toddler, this age is often when children show signs of being ready to leave their nappy behind and join the adults in the toilet, if you see what I mean.

That's right, potty training has arrived – be afraid and on hand with some kitchen towel.

You'll also begin to notice that your little one becomes a much more social being once she turns two. Making friends is a big deal for all of us at any time of life, but these first forays into the world of other people are both interesting and sometimes heartbreaking for you to watch.

What's more, they also begin to gently reinforce that your position, your status if you like has changed forever – you're not just you anymore, you can be and will be often defined as someone's dad – a subtle but important change that will become more profound as your child gets older and as you do, too.

As other children arrive on the scene, either at nursery or on play dates, the odd concept of sharing begins to raise its head.

As British parents, sharing, or the lack of it from our children, is particularly hard to stomach given the almost OCD-like zeal many of us have instilled in us to take a back seat and be selfless.

The sight of our children snatching a toy, reacting with fury and indignation when another child visiting the house dares to play with something that quite clearly belongs to the young master of the premises or – worst of the worst – when our own flesh and blood refuses to wait their turn for the slide and – I can barely even write it – pushes into a queue, all make us determined to get to work asap on bringing them into the 'after you, Claude' fold.

As we will see, though, explaining what sharing is and why it's important to a two-year-old for whom the universe was most definitely created for the sole purpose of spinning round and round them, is a very tricky thing to do indeed.

Finally in these six months the differences that your toddler's gender will make to their personality, development and outlook begin to make themselves known – with the nature and nurture debate at the centre of things as ever.

Perhaps the most profound of occurrences at this time is that thoughts, conversations and glances between you and your partner can all turn to the prospect of adding another member to your family.

With the average gap between children in the UK coming out at around 35 months, this is optimum 'let's start trying again' territory.

Are you ready?

Potty training: keep calm and carry wipes

It probably doesn't seem that long ago that you were fumbling around with your first nappy change, all poo covered thumbs and smeared Sudocrem.

Soon the time to move from nappies to pants will be upon you and your toddler. As well as the practical side of things this transition represents yet another giant leap towards independence.

Before we move into the soggy reality of it all, it's worth asking yourself one question – how many adults do you know who live their lives in giant disposables as a result of their parents having never mastered potty training?

Not many, I hope.

The reason why that's a pertinent point to focus on is that you might find yourself wondering if you and yours will ever crack it; if you will ever be able to travel anywhere again without a bin liner full of clean kids' underwear and a bottle of 1001 carpet cleaner in tow.

But you will, don't worry, you will. Patience and good humour are as important in this little parenting challenge as they are in perhaps any other and besides, it's only poo and wee isn't it, you've practically got a PhD in the pair of them by now anyway.

When are they ready?

This is a key question: go too early and you could be in for a very long haul indeed, with your child forming a stubborn refusal to countenance attempting something that they have found incredibly difficult thus far.

The pressure not to go too late can often come in the form of two things – the first being that some or even all of your child's peers seem to have cracked it already.

The antidote to this, as ever, is so what? As Gary Coleman once said, it takes different strokes to rule the world – and who are we to argue with him? Besides, if you have a son and the dry friends are girls there really is no point even wasting a second's worry on it, because, just for a change, girls tend to get potty training a lot easier than boys.

Poor us.

The other pressure point could well come in the form of a letter from the nursery you are hoping your nipper will attend when they are three. Nestled amongst all the info is often a list of 'things your child must be able to do'.

Just under the alarming-in-its-own-right 'taking off and putting on their own coat' you may well find 'be fully toilet-trained'.

Queue sirens, flashing lights and the purchasing of nine books and five different types of potty contraptions.

Take a breath, relax and have faith, you will get there and a big part of making that happen is attempting to start the process when they are ready rather than when you need them to be ready.

Tragically, that point in time doesn't make itself known via a handwritten note or impassioned speech from your little one, but relies on you spotting some (but rarely all) of the following signs.

> She loves to play at pulling her nappy/pull up/pants up and down. Who doesn't?

> She likes to follow you and/or your partner to the bathroom and even imitate what you do in there.

> She makes a discernible and often unmistakable physical demonstration when a bowel movement is being delivered – this can range from the classic poo face, to an attractive grunt, a give-away squat or even a verbal warning to everyone within range.

> She uses words for stool and urine – hopefully not some of the more colourful ones.

> She seem recognise the physical signals from within that means action is on its way and can tell you about it ahead of time – especially when you are on a bus!

> She actively dislikes the feeling of being in a dirty nappy. There's a theory that children are less likely to be driven to the potty for this reason now most of them are in ultra absorbent disposables rather than soggy, heavy and uncomfortable towelling nappies. I say 'theory', it's what my Dad reckons.

> She has 'dry' periods of at least three or four hours which crucially indicates that the bladder muscles are up to the task of holding and storing urine.

Spot a handful of these and you are in business – but before we move on to what to do, it's worth looking at what *not* to do.

What doesn't work

So you think you've got the green light – time to put the foot down and zoom to a nappy free world.

Not quite.

If toddlers feel undue pressure around potty training it is the easiest thing in the world for them to clam up – literally. They will move through the stages of this in their own time and any attempt to give things a nudge can seriously backfire.

Likewise, when things don't go according to plan and they won't, because they never do, getting frustrated or even angry is to be avoided at all costs, as is any semblance of punishment or rebuke for the many, many accidents you will be cleaning up.

Not only is punishment a complete waste of time, it will have a noticeably negative impact on what you are trying to achieve. Rather than looking forward to a trip to the toilet or the potty they will avoid it at all costs.

Keeping calm and carrying on is the way to go – and even if it's through gritted teeth trying to make – oh dear, never mind – your response of choice is a smart move. Not always easy, but smart.

Much like the world of breastfeeding, you will also find advice on how you can and should approach potty training coming from every corner. If you manage to avoid someone telling you that you are waiting too long or being too soft you will be doing well.

Practices, conventions and techniques have changed on this as on many other fronts – using children as chimney sweeps or to pull coal wagons underground springs to mind – so if you can, smile sweetly and move on. Either that or launch into one and make yourself feel a bit better.

What works

Didn't they do well?

Children love praise.

What am I saying? We all love praise, it's just that children haven't been taught to be coy about showing the fact yet. You'll be amazed what praising the very arse off every little bit of progress and celebrating the merest sniff of success can do.

And I mean really celebrate, go mad, do the David Pleat dance around the front room, the works.

As ever though, if you really do go too far they can be so overwhelmed by your extraordinary reaction that the thought of failure and letting you down can produce such a build-up of pressure that they will wet themselves.

We tread a fine line as parents don't we?

Accidents happen

Has there ever been anyone on the planet who has learnt to drive a manual car without stalling it at least once?

I very much doubt it.

You'll have puddles, you'll have poo parcels, you may even have a trail of both up your cream stair carpet.

C'est la wee.

Open door policy

Toddlers learn by copying, so encourage them to watch. It's probably best that boys watch you and girls watch mum so as not to confuse, but the more they see you both in action the more they will want to do it.

Show-stopping pants and knickers

Take your little one shopping and let them pick whatever underwear they like – children's underwear I mean

Whatever your views on marketing to kids, whatever your principles on television consumption, if purchasing a pack of Iggle Piggle pants or Upsy Daisy knickers will help you motor through potty training just swallow hard, get them bought and hide them straight in your Cath Kidston changing bag.

Make a plan

Defeating the nappy enemy requires some serious military co-ordination. If your youngster is at nursery or with a childminder you'll need them to be on the same page to stand a chance.

Once she has her über underwear you'll need to decide if you are going to set periods of the day in both or go headlong into permanent pant mode and to hell with the consequences and the upholstery. The training pants you'll see in the supermarket get the thumbs-down from many experts because essentially they are still nappies and won't feel wet.

Even better than both in the early potty training skirmishes is to plan in some time when they can get naked (the reason many parents choose to tackle potty training in the summer months). This means there's no barrier whatsoever between your toddler's hind quarters and the floor, but it's a great way for them to really start to learn what it feels like when they need to go.

You will rapidly become an expert in spotting the slightest twitch which signifies they need to go too – the clutch, the hop and, if you're not quick enough, the squat.

There are lots of little ways you can make the whole thing a little more fun. Stack her favourite books next to the potty or toilet or turn to the popular sticker method which sees every success rewarded with another of the adhesive little beauties stuck to a progress chart.

Imagine how much simpler the world would be if adults loved stickers as much as kids did.

If they lose their lustre, you may just have to resort to unadulterated bribery, which normally operates on a sliding scale something like this – raisins, apricots, Percy Pigs, muffin, small toy, large toy, university tuition fees.

Kit

Potties have come a long way.

Some of the ones on the market nowadays look more like Captain Kirk's seat on the bridge than a plastic toilet. As with the pants, if you can engineer it that your tot feels like they own and love their new grown-up gadget, getting them to sit on it will be a whole lot easier.

Although many toddlers are scared of falling into the cavernous toilet, some refuse to demean themselves and sit on a potty and want to do what you do where you do it. If that's the case then an adapter seat is a good buy and can transform the big porcelain hole into a comfy seat perfect for a little bottom. They even manage to retain a smell of wee after only a couple of uses so you can find them in the dark. What will they think of next?

If your child point blank refuses to sit on either the potty or the training seat avoid a stand-off at all costs – act like it's no big deal but keep the potty out and keep talking about it. They will have a go eventually, especially if they see their favourite cuddly toy casually having a wee in it from time to time without so much as a by-your-leave.

Once you've got them sitting down don't rush them, quite the opposite in fact, keep them entertained – the more time they spend on there at this stage the more used to the whole strange affair they will become.

If you have a boy, it makes a lot of sense to start them off by sitting down to do both number ones and twos. We all partake in the luxury of a sit-down wee every now and then, especially when we become knackered dads, so why should we keep it from them? Besides, it's a more straightforward way to learn the basics before they have to master the stand up aim – and we all know how tricky that is.

If you have a girl, try to teach her the front-to-back wipe from a pretty early stage. If this feels too early for her to grasp, then a pat dry technique is a good halfway house.

Into the night

Once you've cracked it and your days have become a dry paradise you can start to tackle night times. Don't be tempted to go too early on this though; much better to really make sure the day is nailed.

Once you think the coast is clear, start keeping an eye on nappies in the mornings and if they are consistently dry put a wipe clean mattress cover under her sheet and give it a whirl. If after a few nights it's obvious their bladder isn't ready to hold tight until the morning, go back to the nappies in a very easy come, easy go way and let her know that you'll try the no-nappy night time game again soon.

Never restrict drinks, but steer away from giving her a massive drink before bed, to give her a fighting chance. You can even wake her up for a 'sleep wee' when you go to bed, too. Staying dry through the night is a tough trick to perfect, so don't worry if you continue to get the odd accident for a good few months or even years after you think you are home and, well, dry.

....

Words from your fellow fathers:

Chris, father of two: *We are still going. . .our daughter is now three-and-three-quarters as she likes to tell us repeatedly. Pity her pooing isn't as good as her fractions.*

To be fair, she's good during the day, but still wearing nappies at night. There's the odd accident and mopping of floors, but very rarely and usually when she's been distracted.

The car seat gets a belting when she's fallen asleep for a while. Bless easy-wash covers.

Tom, father of two: *Potty training was pretty good, some spectacular accidents. The sticker chart did well, with stickers on anything vaguely acceptable as a toilet (except the cat litter).*

My personal horror experience was naturally centred around a poorly tummy, where it just started to slide down her leg. We were in a playground area, Mummy was talking to another mum, and our daughter was very politely trying to communicate there was an issue, sadly for me I spotted it so whisked her to an area to deal with her.

Shit was everywhere, ran out of wipes (of course), flies having a field day, park toilet locked (naturally, what use is that on a FUCKING Saturday?), it was minging.

Rob, father of two: *Multiple accidents for at least two months for us. Poos on the landing. Poos in the bedroom. Poos on the toilet seat!*

Winston, father of two: *One thing you find out when you have kids – they can do massive turds.*

Making friends

For quite a long while, small children just ignore each other.

You arrange play dates, you throw birthday parties, you assemble in the park and each time they manoeuvre round each other like embarrassed guests at a gathering no one wants to be at.

Occasionally they will notice or even acknowledge each other, usually with a hand to the face or a tug of wispy hair – but generally they just aren't that bothered to react – even violently.

Then one day, often after they've got walking really nailed down, they suddenly begin to become social animals. They click with a little pal and before very long they are laughing and chasing and asking when they will see them again.

It's a lovely thing and yet another major physiological and sociological milestone in your child's development from vulnerable babe to proper little person.

In these early exchanges it's more often than not a beautifully simple relationship or two your little one will strike up with a handful of their peers. It revolves around playing and chasing and giggling. The first signs of little in-jokes are sometimes also spied as they seemingly talk semi-gobbledygook to their new mates but end up laughing like drains at whatever it is they have jointly made up.

It's hard to overplay how significant these first fledgling independent interactions are. They represent your child formalising her sense of herself and defining and moulding who they are by the way they interact with other people.

As sweet and lovely as these early stages are, rest assured the complexities that we all know exist as adults around interpersonal relationships and the fact that hell, on occasion, can indeed be other people, do rear their head in the not too distant future for your child.

As time goes on, you'll witness them being rejected and even ridiculed by older kids, having their innocent little overtures and ideas rebuffed and eventually rattling round the school playground on their own on that daunting first morning.

It's hard to describe what all these things do to you as a parent and a father – but suffice to say it's a feeling you won't forget in a hurry. You are essentially witnessing your child learning for the first time that the world and the people in it aren't quite as benevolent, friendly and straightforward as the closeted and loving little environment that they have spent their lives thus far inhabiting.

It really is the first time the fig leaf has fallen away.

On the flip side, they are also becoming alive to the possibility that fun and laughter and excitement can be had in great quantities thanks to the other people they know around them.

Although you're a few months off that yet, now is when that process begins and it's important to clock it – as it is to clock that these social changes in your child's make up also has a subtle but lifelong significance for you and your partner.

Occupation: Daddy

So your child has embarked on her lifelong journey of meeting people – which means you are about to spend the best part of 20 years getting to know other people's children, too.

You'll have your favourites, you'll have ones you can't bear, you'll have ones that make you even more proud of your own children and ones that make you worry about them in comparison.

At this early stage just a month or two either way age-wise can make a huge difference in the dynamic of a fledgling little friendship. In fact you can quite often see a look of total hero worship on your toddler's face for someone six months older and a look of absolute disdain for some poor mite who is the same distance back.

It's just as easy for parents to make judgements too – seeing some kids as good influencers and some as bad. If your child goes to a nursery or playgroup you'll soon be having all sorts of names thrown at you too, rafts of Jacks and Olivias will enter your world as your increasingly chatty little one tells you about her friends.

Where there are other people's children there are other people. Again you'll no doubt take to and take against these new additions to your life as you see fit, but new additions some of them certainly will be as your child spends years in their children's class at school.

And that's what's so important about the start of this little social dance for your tot. It marks the beginning of their interaction with others and the slow start of the process where you are defined by your children and not the other way around.

Think of your friends, some of whom you'll have known for years and years no doubt and the memorable times you've had together.

Now think of their parents, the people who made you vast amounts of dinner, who gave you lifts, who let you have wine like an adult, or who bollocked you for smoking in the garden.

That's you, now, that is.

To every child and parent who comes through your door, from the toddlers now to the teenagers down the line, first and foremost you'll be someone's dad.

What kind of dad is up to you, cool dad, funny dad, angry dad, hide behind the curtains and scare the pants off them dad – the choice is yours – but you will always be a dad now to a whole raft of new people in your life.

Don't let it scare or depress you. The other part of your life, the 'you' part isn't over, it's not gone for good, although it might feel like it at times. It's merely taken a back seat for a while, so you can focus on someone else.

And what's fascinating is that it's through being there for someone other than yourself, through being seen as someone else's father for a while, *that you really find out who you are.*

The weird world of sharing

The advent of friends also brings your child into contact with a new, strange and frustratingly counterintuitive skill they need to master – sharing.

Now none of us is born with the ability to share – and why would we be?

On a strictly Darwinist level, sharing is for losers. In fact up until very recently it's been thought that we humans were the only ones in the entire animal kingdom who exhibited this frankly whacko altruistic behaviour.

A recent study showed that our closest cousins the chimpanzees are capable of sharing, too.[35] Although what scientists didn't discover is whether adult chimps cover their eyes in horror and squeal a thousand apologies when their hairy little offspring snatches a banana off a neighbour's infant.

That's the problem you see, it's we parents who have the big problem with it — especially British parents. I mean, what's more un-British than not waiting your turn? The only thing I can think our children could do that would induce more cringes in us is if they asked every visitor to our house exactly how much they earned – including bonuses – and how they voted in the last general election.

So how should we deal with it?

First, try and disconnect your embarrassment bone. All two- and three-year-olds think they own the world and especially the stuff in their own toy box so they are acting perfectly within type – hitting a behavioural milestone, in fact, by understanding the concept of possession.

'Mine' and 'no' register among the first few words of almost every toddler and for good reason, so don't fret.

The next most important thing to clock is that the journey to help them understand the importance of sharing is a very long one. A quick chat won't do it and you'll think the penny has dropped many a time only to be confronted by a very unsavoury scene over a small red ball.

Practising taking turns during games and play is a good idea, especially if you build in the learning that just because you temporarily give up things, it doesn't mean you'll never see them again.

As with potty training telling your child off for not being a benevolent being is a waste of time at best and counterproductive at worst.

She's not Mahatma Ghandi, it's OK if she wants to keep back her favourite toy and just because there's another parent there to witness it doesn't mean that you are compelled to make an example of her. Rather, when she does share something let her know that you think she's just done a very great thing indeed.

When she gets a bit older, it can be well worth exploring the emotional side of how she feels when someone else plays with her stuff. Talk about how it can make her feel sad and let her know that you understand. Be careful this exercise doesn't boomerang back on you though, otherwise the next time someone borrows your pen at work you might find yourself pulling everything off your desk in a rage against the injustice of it all and giving the water cooler a series of violent kicks.

As ever, a big part of learning will come through seeing what you do. So when you give her some of your drink, let her know you are sharing with her, or don't just tell her a story or a secret, share it with her instead – that way she will come across this odd little concept often and realise that it isn't just her that has her civil liberties infringed, it happens to all of us.

....

Words from your fellow fathers

Chris, father of two: *Sharing still depends on the mood of my eldest. Sometimes she's the UN peace keeping force. Other times she's out to conquer the world and own everything.*

In general a good sharer, especially with other kids at playschool, not so much with her sister.

Winston, father of two: *There is the middleclass dance parents do when they make their child give everything they are holding, even their dearest toy, to the toddler who is visiting. 'No Jacob, let Tabitha play with Mr Snuffy.'*

Sometimes it might be best to let them work it out for themselves.

Marcus, father of four: *Four children in a very short period of time solved any sharing problems.*

Boys and girls

As your toddler has begun to grow and develop you'll have noticed that she has left the homogenised and limited repartee of the baby behind her and started to exhibit and exhort herself as an individual.

Oh yes, you'll have noticed that all right by now.

Many factors help to shape your child's character – genetics, environment, diet all play their part.

But as she grows, it's obvious that one factor in particular shows its hand more than most – gender.

As little boys swoop around the garden arms outstretched in jet mode and become obsessive about steam trains that even their grandparents struggle to remember first-hand, you begin to ask yourself, have we made this happen or is it just in them?

Then, in some ways even more starkly given the changing role of the modern women, when your little girl loves nothing more than putting her soft toys to bed and vacuuming with her replica appliance you (and especially your partner perhaps) will be amazed at how conformist these little people seem to be to the old school gender stereotypes that have been far from pushed on them.

This in itself is a generalisation. Plenty of boys love doing 'girl' things and vice versa, but the fact remains that there's more to this nature and nurture debate then just making sure you miss out the sexist bits in any Enid Blyton you read to them.

So other than the obvious ones, what are the actual differences that are playing out in front of you and what's going on in their little hearts, bodies and minds?

The physical side

Although boys and girls grow at roughly the same rate up until early adolescence when girls spurt first, only for boys to catch up and often pass them a year or two later, there are significant differences in the way their motor skills develop.

For boys the macro or gross skills like balancing, jumping and running often kick in slightly earlier, while girl's fine skills like writing develop sooner. This is one of the reasons why girls often speed ahead in early education (often never to be caught up, if the stats are to be believed).

When boys take physical risks, the pleasure centre of their brains lights up like a Christmas tree and they get a thrill, which explains why if you're a parent of a little man you will be kept very busy as they impulsively explore and push boundaries.

The stereotypical story goes that little boys are harder when they are young, crashing, bashing and breaking everything in their path, while girls sit and colour in for hours on end. Then, when the teenage years come around boys become straightforward and easier but girls are transformed into mega stroppy handfuls.

There's even a term coined on Mumsnet, SMOGs – Smug Mothers of Girls – to neatly encapsulate those for whom the early years of parenting apparently breeze by in a whirr of pink princesses and peaceful play. A counterinsurgency group DMOBs – Defensive Mums of Boys – has even sprung up.

I'll leave you to decide what you make of this war of the young roses being played out online, but you can't help feeling that if someone were to actually state that all small girls *should* be quiet and timid while all small boys fearless and inquisitive they would rightly get shot down as displaying gender prejudice of the worst kind.

Communication

Verbally, most girls get the gift of the gab earlier than boys, and boys use fewer words on average. Girls have also been seen to be better at clocking non-verbal signals like tone of voice and expression, which play a huge part in them being overall better early communicators than their male peers. Pointing out the emotions felt by characters in books and indeed felt by themselves is a good idea no matter what the sex of your child, but for boys in particular it's a great way of helping them to kick start that part of their make-up.

Pink brain, blue brain?

As we've mentioned, discourage gender stereotypes as you might, some will still sprout and flourish before your eyes – for instance boys love guns, they just bloody love them, you can ban them from your house if you like but the TV remote, the clothes pegs, the fingers on his hand, you can't ban them.

Why is that – do boys and girls have different brains?

Scientists suspect that might be the case.

There might be, for instance, a part of a boy's brain that makes moving objects, like wheels and balls, utterly fascinating and beguiling and another part of a girl's grey matter that drives them toward pushing a plastic baby round the living room in a toy pram for hours and hours on end, to nurture.

It's often postulated by armchair anthropologists that this is a throwback to our savannah days, when survival depended on men stalking the moving beasts of the plain and women keeping those same beasts away from the children.

They could be right.

Research[36] into enduring mystery of the 'blue for a boy and pink for a girl' world in which we live recently found that women do seem to be hard wired to preferring the pinks and lilac end of the colour spectrum because in our hunter gatherer days the ability to tell an edible ripe berry from a potentially poisonous one relied on the ability to grade those types of hues.

What's for certain is that some areas of the brain grow faster in females than in males and vice versa and that this process begins straight from birth.

Research has shown[37] that in girls, the language and emotion parts of the brain is bigger as is the area that connects the left and right lobes, we males on the other hand have been found to have a slightly bigger deeper emotion centre which looks after things like fear. Brilliant.

Let's not get too fatalistic about this whole boy-brain-girl-brain thing, though.

It's worth remembering as a parent that the old adage that your brain is a muscle that must be exercised like any other turns out to be very true indeed, especially in the young. Key areas can expand or shrink depending on how they are used – so despite the odd bit of predetermined hard wiring there's plenty of room for them being what they want and thinking what they want.

Aren't babies brilliant? Thinking about trying for the next one?

The sleep deprivation has passed, kind of, the muslins are all but packed away and the carry cot is full of toys.

You need another baby!

Well, you *might* do. Although two children remains the most common family size in the UK, the number of only children is on the rise. In 1972, 18% of the nation's children had the toybox all to themselves, while the latest figures show that more than a quarter of all the UK's children are living without siblings.[38]

The reason for that seems to be multilayered, with finance and the number of couples already feeling like they are stretching themselves very thin indeed as they both juggle full-time jobs and a child, both being cited.

We all know the lazy stereotypes bandied around about only children – spoilt, bossy oddballs who struggle their entire lives to form well-balanced relationships because they could always watch what they wanted on the telly.

As ever with these kind of myths it's possible to trace it back to a single point, in this case according to Susan Newman, a social psychologist and author of *Parenting an Only Child*, to the late 1800s when G. Stanley Hall, known as the founder of child psychology, labelled being an only child 'a disease in itself'.

Newman adds that there:

> *'. . .have been hundreds and hundreds of research studies that show that only children are no different from their peers.'[39]*

As well as the effect of keeping it to just the one has on the child itself, there's also the emotional pull felt by mums and dads alike. Put simply, many of us just want to do it all again. Despite the undoubted difficulties, the chronic sleep deprivation and the loss of great swathes of our former lives – despite how we may moan about it on occasion – being a parent is an experience like no other and to many the thought of only feeling that the once is inconceivable.

Call it greedy breeding if you like, and many do in the world of diminishing resources on which we find ourselves spinning, but for millions of us it's an innate drive that doesn't have an off switch.

There is no absolute guarantee that just because you and your partner have conceived once, you will definitely be able to do it again. Secondary infertility as it's called is thought by some experts to be on the increase[40] and even more common than primary infertility – with the later age that couples are choosing to start their families pointed to as part of the cause.

But if you've both decided that you do want another and if you are lucky enough to be able to conceive another you've got two key questions to answer: Can we afford it? And what is the best age gap to leave between our children?

Finance

I hope you're sitting down.

Research carried out in 2011 found that on average parents will spend £271,499 on each child up to the age of 21.[41]

Just take a moment if you need one.

As a result of that bowel-opening figure the same survey found that 58% of parents surveyed with only one child said they are weren't planning to have any more.

Now it's all very well and good to say that vulgar and coldly pragmatic factors like cost shouldn't come into such an emotional and profound decision like having another baby or not, but at more than a quarter of a million pounds a pop you'd be mad, impetuous, love-flooded fools not to at least give it some serious thought – especially given the financial black hole the planet finds itself in.

There are savings to be made and compromises to be struck, but even if you make your brood make do with a satsuma at Christmas and have them run everywhere to save on petrol, you're still looking at hundreds of thousands of pounds that you'll need to find over the next two decades.

Like most couples who have more than one child, you'll probably do the sums, scratch your head and think, 'we'll manage'. Your next decision is what you see as the optimal age difference between your offspring.

Mind the gap

According to the Office for National Statistics the average interval between births in England and Wales is 35 months – which as it happens is just about exactly the gap that research has suggested is best for both children and parents.[42]

In truth there are pros and cons to whatever age gap you choose, although medical opinion is pretty undivided on the fact that waiting at least 18 months before having your next one allows the mother's body to recover from the battering it has just been through and also reduces the risk of the next baby being premature or underweight.

In terms of reducing the threat of sibling rivalry there's no doubt that having your second before your first is two years old can have a positive effect, primarily because the older child hasn't really developed a fully rounded sense of identity yet so is less likely to feel full rounded jealousy.

But having two babies in the house, neither really capable of entertaining themselves, or potentially sleeping through the night and both still in nappies must be incredibly hard work. For a while you'd essentially have twins (if your second actually turned out to be twins, life, as you know it, would be over.) As time goes on, because they are close in age they stand more of a chance of playing well together earlier. So you takes your choice.

Sibling rivalry can be at its most intense when the age gap between children is around the two-year mark. Frustrated and short of fuse anyway, the arrival of an interloper who halves the attention they receive at best can go down very badly indeed. Again though, once you've got through the tough few years you could well have a couple of lifelong playmates on your hands.

With a gap of three years or above the chances of sibling rivalry slackens off again with emotional maturity of the older sibling helping them to cope with the new arrival and often enjoy it.

There's also a sense with a 36-month gap that you've somehow had the time to enjoy the first child properly and give them the attention they need. It also gives both parents a taste of their old life back; work, friends, sleep, all make a gentle return.

For some this is a good thing, for others it's a tease, a nostalgic dream sequence that will soon be snuffed out as they are plunged back into new-born babydom.

While there's no hard and fast answer to the best gap to choose, the fact that for once research and actual activity chime, may well point to the fact that the parental herd have decided that the two-to-three-year gap feels best all round. Given that your partner was probably capable of conceiving just a handful of months after the birth of your first child you may well be reading this expecting your second already.

Good luck.

....

Words from your fellow fathers

Chris, father of two: *We were both up for number two and we started trying fairly soon after. Unfortunately we lost two pregnancies both at about three months. Possibly the most traumatic, emotional time of my life to date. I could see it nearly destroyed my wife and it's been a long road back – all that hope, that happiness at finding out you're pregnant, all destroyed in an instant, and then back on the same rollercoaster.*

I remember the second one I was super positive, and thought I had a gut feeling that it'd be fine. Maybe I just didn't want to consider the alternative. But my wife is a vet, and as the doctor waved the ultrasound around, she could 'read' what was on the screen whereas I couldn't. She knew before the doctor even said anything. It was devastating.

The only thing that brought us all back was try number three that came through to become our beautiful daughter – and that three-month check was as nervous as I've ever been.

Mark, father of one: *Our second is due soon – we pretty much had to forget how tiring it all was and look back with rose-tinted glasses to build up the courage, but we're getting old and we didn't want to wait too long or we would never do it.*

Tom, father of two: *We were both equally up for having our second.*

The only disappointment was how quickly it happened vs the first. It was a bit like when you play a child at pool, you quickly

*find yourself with all your stripes down, and desperately want to
play it out so the child can eventually win.*

*Then, while snookered beyond belief, you manage to pot the
black.*

Your progress report

Your baby

Your child's Tellytubby-like shape that you have become so used to
seeing wibbling and wobbling around your house may well begin
to change now.

As well as the lengthening of her arms and legs as she grows, the
sheer amount of calories burnt on a daily basis as she gets up to
all sorts will mean that some of her puppy fat will disappear before
your eyes.

What with tantrums, exploration and the fact that every single
day brings something new and wondrous to their little lives
you will have a very tired soldier on your hands come the end of
the day.

Hopefully you've managed to cling on to the lunchtime nap
which will help get her through the day, but even with that, she
need to kip and kip long of a night time. If for whatever reason she
has a broken or shortened night you will know about it in a big
way the next day.

All of which means, despite swearing years ago that you'd never
do it when you were on the receiving end, you will slowly but
surely turn into a 'time for bed' parent.

It comes to us all.

You and your partner

Leaving aside the 'let's have another one' debate and the fact that the ever-present exhaustion is still ever present, this is often a period to be savoured for both of you.

Forget the much-mentioned tantrums, you've got an endlessly inquisitive, impossibly cute and relentlessly enthusiastic ray of sunshine in your house for the most part.

You'll be truly amazed how quickly the time will come when you are waving your baby goodbye at the school gate for the first time, with a lump in your throat and enough mixed emotions in your head and heart to make you dizzy.

Cliché though it is, you'll never get these moments back, so when you find yourself debating whether to leave early or take a cheeky half day, do it, it's only work after all. Soaking up every minute you can of your two-year-old is a better use of your time in so many ways.

Months 31-36
Bye bye, baby

So we have nearly reached the end of our journey from newborn to nursery.

The helpless little baby you gingerly brought home nearly three years ago – yes three years ago – is now a fully-fledged member of your family and imagining life without her is nigh on impossible.

As well as having opinions and questions – lots of questions – she will also be developing a lovely little sense of humour. As well as being a joy to behold, not to mention the beginnings of a captive and receptive audience to your jokes, humour is an important part of your toddler's development and brings with it all sorts of benefits and learnings – as if just having a laugh wasn't good enough in itself.

Slightly less funny is having a fussy eater on your hands as many parents do. A baby who throws everything hither and thither is one thing, a headstrong three-year-old who refuses to eat 99% of what is put in front of her is quite another and can cause real worry and stress.

If you've decided to double the size of your family and a new arrival is on the way you might also be anxious about how child number two will be received by current king of the hill number one. It can be a tricky one, but the good news is there are some practical things you can do to lessen the impact and even turn it into something they genuinely look forward to, rather than resent the very mention of.

Quite often this age can be a time of big change for your toddler, not just because of the arrival of a brother or sister, but also because that big event coincides with another – starting nursery. With all three- and four-year-olds entitled to 15 hours of free nursery education for 38 weeks of the year, many a little one makes their first foray into structured childcare – some even putting on a uniform to do it, which will make you proud and sad in equal measure.

If watching your child playing at nursery for the first time doesn't make the point perfectly you'll realise you really are saying goodbye to your baby when they turn three.

Group hug.

Knock knock: humour and your child

Making a baby smile is one of life's little joys and when you stop to think about it they learn to express their pleasure at an astonishingly early stage in their development.

Making a noise or pulling a face to generate a gummy grin soon moves on to games like peek-a-boo that mildly shock, but because the surprise comes from a trusted source like you or your partner the incongruity tickles them pink.

It's that ability to first recognise and then compute that something unusual or out of the ordinary has just happened that comes to the fore as they move into toddlerhood.

First it's often based around physicality. Daddy with Nana's glasses on! Why, that is hilarious. Mummy pretending to drop a toy on the floor? Priceless.

It may not be award-winning comedy but it's far from a simple process you're witnessing when your toddler gets things like that and falls about. First she needs to know what's normal before they can spot what's not.

Then research has shown[43] that before she cracks up she needs to be able to tell that the action is a deliberate mistake or exaggeration. It is essentially a very early introduction to the notion that an action can have more than one meaning – which is a complex concept indeed for someone who still can't wipe their own bottom properly.

Once her vocabulary gets that bit more wide-ranging, she will start reacting to words that pop up in the wrong place, or seem to.

'The juice is in the *bottom* of the bag' could, on any given day, reduce a three-year-old to pant-wetting hysterics. Not only does that represent the continuation for another generation of the fine and longstanding obsession we have in this country with toilet humour, it is also word play, pure and simple.

As well as being just lovely to be around, this blossoming sense of humour really is something to be encouraged because it brings with it some tangible benefits.

As well as helping her to see things from different perspectives and beyond their face value she also develops the confidence to respond spontaneously to situations.

You'll probably have noticed that toddlers often take themselves and their problems really quite seriously. Intense some might call them on occasion. Well, as their sense of humour starts to really come together at this age it can be a real ally. Making a toddler laugh as she teeters on the precipice of a major meltdown can have miraculous effects.

As she grows up, a well-developed sense of humour, as we all know, is a fantastic thing to have in her arsenal – from making her generally happier to being better able to handle the slings and arrows of outrageous fortune that life launches at her.

As well as the obvious benefits, medical evidence of the physical and mental pluses laughter brings continues to mount.[44] From stimulating your major organs and muscle groups thanks to your increased intake of oxygen-rich air to pacifying your stress response laughter, if not the best medicine, is certainly right up there with penicillin and chocolate.

So what can you do to help your child grow up loving to laugh? Well, being funny yourself is a good start. No pressure, of course.

You don't have to be that funny, it is small children we are talking about. As audiences go, they are on your side as you are already one of the two funniest people they have ever met – but just remember to be a bit silly and laugh out loud, even when you are having the week from hell.

Also, making a point of recognising and encouraging your child's early attempts at humour is a great idea. As a man you will know for a fact that there are very few feelings on the planet with the ability to make you feel as good about yourself as having someone laugh at your jokes.

You can also help to create a humour-rich environment by getting really involved in the books they read, there are some seriously funny children's titles out there. If you are stuck, check out the inspired nonsense that comedy legend Spike Milligan wrote for his kids – it will have you both laughing out loud.

The only pitfall to look out for on this front is that learning when humour *isn't* appropriate is actually quite tricky – or at least, I find it tricky. So when they put the whoopy cushion under your aunty with the heart condition, or decide to end everything they say, all day, with the word poo, go easy on them, it's just a joke!

Fussy eaters

Fussy eating isn't funny.

If you've got a picky toddler at your dinner table every day you'll know that it can be a hugely stressful and upsetting situation to tackle.

It must be something to do with the very basic need we have as parents to make sure our offspring are well fed, but watching them refuse one thing after another can get to you in a way few other things do – to the extent that some parents actively dread mealtimes and the futile battle of the bowl they must once again wage.

As soon as the little person in the high chair gets wind that you are getting vexed about the whole thing, she will clamp her lips together tighter than ever and wave dish after dish away like a disgusted food critic.

The trick, hard though it may be for you and your partner to pull off, is to breathe deeply, pull a smile from somewhere and take the heat out of the situation. As dire as it may feel this, like so many other things you think will be lifelong afflictions, will pass in the fullness of time.

Part of the problem is often the empty plate syndrome. We parents love nothing more than to see every speck of grub devoured, but we often don't give enough thought to the size of the stomach we are trying to fill or the portion size that would accomplish it.

The result is a toddler confronted with a relative mountain of food and a parent disheartened that they've not finished it.

If your child keeps their mouth shut half way through a meal, shakes their head, says no, pushes the spoon away, squirrels food in their mouth and refuses to swallow it, tries desperately to get out of the high chair or begins to gag or retch – guess what, they have probably had enough.

As obvious as that sounds, it's amazing how easy it is for a parent to ignore signs that from an adult would be as conclusive as can be and put them down to mischief or misguidedness just because they come from an infant.

Aside from keeping an eye out for them just being full, there are things you can do to encourage your toddler to broaden their horizons a little and take the brave step away from yoghurt and toast towards a world of nutritious and exciting eating possibilities.

Like almost everything in their lives, when you place a new food in front of a toddler they are almost certainly seeing and smelling it for the first time. While some youngsters barely let it hit the plate before devouring it, others sniff, prod and poke at it as if they are expecting it to come alive and run off at any moment.

They need time to learn that the food you put in front of them is safe and enjoyable – some do this in a split second, others take months and even years. Be careful not to fall into the trap of thinking a certain food is off limits just because they have refused it a couple of times. Bring it out a few weeks later with a flourish and she might just tuck in.

Arranging a daily routine for meals and eating together as a family or occasionally with her little friends can be a good idea too. Once sees how much everyone else loves sprouts, she could well be encouraged to try them herself, maybe.

Making finger foods part of meal times can make a difference as can putting a sheet down and letting her make as much mess as she likes. If you put her in the bath and told her to sit perfectly still while she was washed she would probably start to refuse to do that too. Make it fun.

Talking of which, when you have a bit of time, take her shopping, get her to choose her food and then ask her to help you make it. It's not just bosses who need to feel ownership of things. If your child thinks she has been part of the decision-making process around meal times, she is much more likely to end up with food in her mouth than on the floor.

Praise, as ever, is your best friend. Treat the digesting of one pea like a major lottery win and adorn your toddler with kisses and stickers and resist the temptation to end the moment on a downer by then loading up the fork with 35 more of the green demons.

A little pitfall to be aware of and one that I must have stumbled into hundreds of times before I cottoned on is to give a drink before or with her meal. Several glugs later I'd have an empty glass and a little boy who was full of liquid.

If things get really bad and you or your partner start to actually make a reserve meal for when the first is refused, you need to rein things back. Once your toddler realises all they need to do to have their food replaced is turn their nose up, you will soon be running a Yo Sushi carousel for one very picky customer.

Likewise the old threat of withholding the pudding if the savoury isn't eaten has always struck me as a sure-fire way for kids to begin life thinking that anything that isn't sweet is inferior. Don't be afraid to try them on things you are convinced they won't like, or because you don't like them and don't be afraid to do a bit of rebranding.

Fried calamari? Never.

Octopus chips? Gimme, gimme, gimme.

Finally, don't feel guilty or down if one mealtime turns into a nightmare. Go again next time full of enthusiasm and optimism. They can smell a doom-laden situation a mile off, these three-year-olds.

If things continue to be difficult and you become seriously worried about how much she is taking in, or if you suspect she has lost any weight, make a list of all the food and drink that has passed her lips over the course of a week and go and chat to your GP.

Chances are the problem isn't anywhere near as grave as you thought and the doctor will helpfully tell you that you've got a fussy eater on your hands.

Thanks, Doc.

....

Words from your fellow fathers

Simon, father of one: *Our boy isn't a bad eater at all – he eats the same as us where practical. I was very keen to get him eating grown-up stuff like olives, garlic, etc. Don't know why, all he really likes is garden peas!*

Jason, father of two: *Our eldest was good in the early years and respected his Irish and Sri Lankan roots by gobbling potatoes and rice.*

At three he eats sausages, olives and not much else.

Tom, father of two: *I made several vats of things, 20 ice cube trays worth. I was a bit gutted at the rejection of my 'cod, spinach and potato' number, particularly so as it became my work lunches for a few times. Man, was it plain.*

Getting ready for your new baby

Bringing a new baby back to your home, a home which is now your toddler's personal castle, can be very tricky.

It doesn't have to be a nightmare and you could be pleasantly amazed by how loving and accepting your eldest child is, but there's always a chance that every cuddle will turn into a vice-like bear hug and every seemingly gentle stroke into a poorly disguised poke.

It's understandable, though, isn't it?

You've poured affection and attention into your eldest in quite staggering amounts, you've told them that they are the most beautiful thing in the whole wide world on a daily basis and you've fallen in love with them hook, line and sinker.

Then along comes another one and halves it all. Although it probably doesn't feel like half to them, no matter how many 'proud brother or sister' balloons you give them – it must be a very strange thing for them to get their head around.

You can help them, though. There are ways and means of softening the blow and even getting them excited. First, don't be tempted to tell them you are expecting a brother or sister too early. Nine months is an eternity for a toddler and the more time you give them to mature and grow the better chance you have of them computing the news that bit better.

Once you do spill the beans and tell her that there is a baby growing inside Mummy's tummy, be aware how utterly mindblowing and bizarre the news must sound to them.

A baby, one of those things in the pushchairs, growing in Mummy's tummy, GROWING IN A TUMMY!

Not only will they struggle with the biology of it all – and I'm not sure I fully understand it – they will have no idea of the changes a second baby will bring to their lives.

And neither will you.

Tell them that the baby can hear them, which after a few months is true, and encourage them to talk to their brother or sister and even get some photos out of them when they were tiny so they can visualise this new thing in their lives.

It's tempting to talk about the new baby being a playmate for them, which will indeed get them excited, until they are presented with the non-talking, non-moving, non-anything bundle in a few months' time and quite simply think it's rubbish.

As the birth approaches, there are some good children's books that address this issue out there. Getting your toddler involved in the preparations can be a smart move, too, and make them feel really involved and grown-up.

Letting them choose a present for their brother or sister is a similarly bond-inducing exercise and if when they first meet the baby the little mite has also remembered to bring a present for them, well that would be just fantastic and start everyone on a good footing.

The first meeting between the two is much discussed and probably over-analysed. There's one school of thought that says never let your toddler catch first sight of their new sibling when it's in Mummy's arms. Legend has it that this will leave an indelible imprint on them from which they will never recover.

What's for sure is that if your partner has been away from your older child for a few days in hospital she will want to hug her to within an inch of her life once they are reunited so for that reason alone it's probably best if the baby is in the cot rather than her arms.

A word to the wise, if your older is still in a cot at home, a cot that you need for the new one on the way, it's best to make the move to the big bed before the baby is anywhere near the point where she will essentially turf their older sibling out on their ear.

Once the baby is born, it's inevitable they will get a lot of attention. Everyone loves a baby and the cooing and fussing can be hard for your toddler to stomach so be alive to it. If necessary ask relatives who come to visit to make a fuss of both of them – any of them who have had children themselves will almost certainly know the score on this having lived it themselves.

While any contact your toddler has with the newborn will need to be strictly and closely supervised, it's important not to appear hugely over-protective of the baby. Up until now the only person they have seen you care that much about is them so try and be sensitive to how you come across.

Watching a toddler 'hold' a newborn, even with you in ultra-close attendance, can be one of life's more nerve-wracking experiences, but if you ban all contact between the two it is very hard for any kind of relationship, no matter how fledgling, to develop between them.

Having said that you should never leave the two of them alone together, no matter how mature or pleased with the baby they seem to be.

With your partner having just given birth and concentrating on feeding and bonding with her new child you have an important role to play. Some fathers see what was a quite frosty, mummy-focussed infant suddenly become dad's best friend and some long-lasting bonds can be formed in this early spell.

Making some special time to be with your toddler on her own, just playing and talking and listening, can really work wonders. It gives your partner a break to get to grips with early motherhood again, and it can strengthen and deepen your relationship with your child at a time when they need it most.

The tricky thing is, that even with paternity leave, time will be at a premium for you because you, my friend, will have another baby in the house!

What's having two like?

We are all men of the world so I'll give it to you straight.

It's very hard indeed.

As a couple you become pulled in either one of two directions – neither of which is towards each other. Sleep deprivation returns like a long-lost friend except this time rather than being able to catch a few zzzzzs when the baby dozes through most of the day, you'll have a toddler with 10 hours of sleep in them demanding you build that obstacle course you promised.

And that's just you. Your partner will be seriously under the cosh and needs all the help she can get. All the preparation tips you hear but never do before your first baby are now essential – freeze lots of meals, never turn down help and let the finer points of housework go hang for a few weeks.

Speaking as one of seven children I literally have no clue how my parents kept us and themselves alive. None.

All I can imagine is that there were a spate of mild winters, they had the capacity to survive on the equivalent of one night's sleep spread across the entire year (a gift they have not passed on to me) or that somehow the 60s and 70s existed across a different time dimension that meant children spent the first decade of their lives in a kind of sedentary stasis – growing but never moving or talking.

Either that or previous generations were just hard and we patently aren't.

Of course, you will survive the arrival of your second, you learn to cope and turn it into a new version of normality just as you did when your first one arrived and catapulted your world upside down.

What's on your side this time is that you've already been there once. You'll both be less panicky and more measured as you recognise scenarios that sent you off the deep end first time round but are met with no more than a knowing smile now.

You'll still be beyond knackered though.

....

Words from your fellow fathers

Winston, father of two: *The age gap of around two-and-a-half years, so far, works very well, in that the older child is mature enough to accept another child and understand, while the younger one is close enough in age to be of interest to the first.*

To walk in a room and hear them giggling together is a thing of joy. It is normally because one is sat on the other, squashing them.

Jason, father of two: *No real jealousy between the boys, just mummy envy from me, she was in demand.*

Tom, father of two: *I wanted a third, she didn't. The business has now officially ceased trading. I'm cool with that.*

Saying goodbye to your baby

So here we are, at the end of our story.

Everyone involved in our little journey from newborn to nursery has come a very long way since the nervous drive home from the hospital.

Your baby started out as an utterly dependent being who looked and acted, let's be honest, so undercooked that she felt like she could have done with another six months in the oven-like womb to warm through thoroughly.

But once she got her bearings, found out where the milk was coming from and got on with the business of growing, she has transformed at an astonishing rate into the bobbydazzler you see before you.

Your partner has seen herself transformed too; a whole new way to be and feel has buried itself deep in her psyche and the emotions, impulses and beliefs that motherhood has instilled in her will be with her forever.

And you?

You have become a father, not just a 'new dad' or a mother's helper, but a father. There's a long way to go and many more moments of joy and pain to experience, but by the time your child reaches three you have at least begun to understand just what a responsibility and a blessing it is to have someone call you Daddy.

All right, so you can't go out and enjoy yourself as often, or put as much into your job as you used to, but the truth is your children will give you more enjoyment than you know what to do with in the coming years if you let them.

As for work, this is the hardest, most important project you'll ever take on – anything else is primarily just paying the bills.

The third year of your child's life can bring with it a change in tone and environment for many parents with nursery entering the picture. While it's not exactly packing the kids off to boarding school there's no doubt that when your baby starts their first day on the long educational road – even when this first step is a very gentle one – you will feel the sands of time passing incredibly quickly as they come home with tales of best friends and songs sung, of fallings out and races won.

The little one you've carried around, cuddled and wiped the bottom of will be making a big move towards independence and while you'll no doubt feel pleased and proud at the progress they make, it hurts a little bit too as they need you that little bit less.

Having just experienced my eldest son's first day at proper school I can confirm that those mixed feelings continue for a while yet – and I have an inkling that they may never fully disappear.

But let's not get too tearful. We've got years of being there for them ahead of us so let's resolve to enjoy and savour as much of it as we possibly can. Let's also give ourselves and our partners the credit we deserve and not, in this age of the micro manager, fret about every decision we make or judgement we might get wrong.

It's worth remembering that not so very long ago life used to be about survival and that while the luxury of time we have been given can bring with it a host of benefits, we can also think, ponder and analyse ourselves to a standstill.

You are right in the thick of the best, most important thing you'll ever do, enjoy it.

So here's to fathers' intuition and the trusting of it – and here's to you and your family.

....

Final words from your fellow fathers

Colin, father of two: *We recently took our daughter for her first day at nursery – I was in BITS. Cried, no, sobbed all the way to work.*

Ben, father of two: *The best thing about being a father is looking at your growing family and thinking how wonderful it is to love and be loved.*
This feeling is increased tenfold if your children are all asleep.

Chris, father of two: *The best part of it all is cuddles and laughter with your kids. Just having them there in your life – it is indescribable how such small simple things that they do, or say, or the way they look at you, can cast so much sunshine in your life. They enable you to truly feel love. And they turn grown men into sops.*

Jason, father of two: *My eldest son says the best thing about being a dad is being able to play on the computers.*
I say it's the best thing that happened to me.

Your progress report

Your baby

It's tempting, especially if a second baby has arrived, to expect your three-year-old to never put a foot wrong. Compared with the newborn she will seem like a fully grown adult, but they are still tiny little things.

In fact your toddler becomes a bit of a sensitive soul at this stage and is quite aware of other people's moods and emotional states and might be curious as to why Mummy is sad or why Daddy is laughing.

Being as open and honest as you can is almost always the best bet – although explaining that the panicked look on your face is due to the fact that as a family you are very close to the breadline and unless you find a bag of used tenners in the street soon you will have to sell the dog, is probably worth giving a miss.

Encouraging her to feel comfortable talking about her feelings and fostering the sense that it's completely normal to have different emotions is a great habit to get into – and might even teach you a thing or two.

With nursery round the corner your child will come into contact with all sorts of new feelings and situations as she becomes even more of a social being. Helping her to be attuned and at home to her own emotions as well as those of others is a real gift you can help to give her.

Also on the cerebral front your house might get a visit from an imaginary friend at this age.

If an invisible playmate does turn up, don't panic and call in the shrinks, it's not only normal, it's actually very creative.

Often it is also a way children make distinctions between good and bad, by using their friend as the one who is responsible for naughty things that she may have done herself or for playing out scenarios to see what would happen without having to do it for real.

They sound good these imaginary friends, don't they – we should all have one.

Try not to make a big deal of her friend either by bursting her imaginary bubble or, conversely, by embracing them too wholeheartedly and losing your marbles.

As with a lot of these things if you are worried about how long your new guest will stay think how many adults you know with a pretend pal – other than David Cameron's made-up mate Nick, not that many.

You and your partner

Now that your baby is all grown-up and reaching her third birthday, she now officially becomes your best mate.

She will still have her moments but all in all it's astonishing just how grown-up three-year-olds are nowadays. Whether it's a good or a bad thing is a moot point but I'm pretty sure we weren't up to, or in to, half as much as they are when we were infants.

You'll find yourself having proper conversations with them now and you will definitely be able to see traits from both you and your partner coming through loud and clear – most of them good, some of them making you realise that you need to be very careful what you do and say in front of them.

Outbursts in the car, arguments at home, they are all fair game and hearing your toddler repeat something you'd rather they didn't is one of life's low points.

That little pitfall aside, you begin to get a real glimpse of the person you have helped to create at this age and just how much enjoyment, love, pride and friendship you can benefit from as they continue to grow.

You and your partner have put an awful lot into getting your baby this far and you should be proud. From now on in your child will be increasingly paying you back for your efforts with interest. The things she says, the things she does, the hugs she gives and the privilege of being able to see a unique little person developing at such close quarters will bring so much to your life that the memories of the sleepless nights will fade away to nothing as your heart is filled with pride and love for the special little person you have both brought into being.

Good work.

References

All websites accessed 28 November 2011.

1. *Guardian*. Midwives condemn 'campaign against home births'.
29 December 2010. www.guardian.co.uk/lifeandstyle/2010/dec/29/
midwives-campaign-home-births

2. Morris, Desmond, *Babywatching*. (London: Jonathan Cape, 1991)

3. BBC News. Breastfed babies 'develop fewer behaviour problems'. 10
May 2011. www.bbc.co.uk/news/health-13336986

4. Womenshealth.gov. Breastfeeding. 4 August 2011. www.
womenshealth.gov/breastfeeding/why breastfeeding-is-important

5. *The Times*. Benefits of breastfeeding 'being oversold by the NHS'.
20 July 2009. www.timesonline.co.uk/tol/life_and_style/health/
article6719696.ece

6. www.dunstanbaby.co.uk

7. BBC News. Post natal depression in fathers 'often undiagnosed'. 18
May 2010. http://news.bbc.co.uk/1/hi/health/8687189.stm

8. *Mail Online*. Crying babies are at risk of brain damage, claims child
expert. 23 April 2010. www.dailymail.co.uk/news/article 1267977/
Crying-babies-risk-brain-damage-claims child-expert-Dr-Penelope-
Ford.html

9. *The Telegraph*. 'Breadwinner Wives' now number 2.7m. 31 January
2010. www.telegraph.co.uk/news/uknews/7120411/Breadwinner-
wives-now-number-2.7m.html

10. *Guardian*. Social changes across the globe. 28 April 2011. www.
guardian.co.uk/news/datablog/2011/apr/28/fertility-rates-social-
change-data

11. BBC News. Stay-at-home fathers 'up 10-fold'. 6 April 2010. http://
news.bbc.co.uk/1/hi/education/8605824.stm

12. World Health Organization. Early Child Development. August 2009. www.who.int/mediacentre/factsheets/fs332/en/index.html

13. Huttenlocher *et al.*, 1991, and Hart and Risley, 1995, cited in Shonkoff, Jack, Phillips, Deborah (eds). *From Neurons to Neighborhoods: The science of early childhood development.* (Washington, DC: National Academies Press, 2000). www.nap.edu/openbook. php?isbn=0309069882&page=137

14. Arnetminer. Do you speak E-N-G-L-I-S-H? A comparison of foreigner and infant-directed speech. 2007. www.arnetminer.org/viewpub.do?pid=1143193

15. Werner, Emmy, Smith, Ruth. *Overcoming the Odds: High-risk children from birth to adulthood.* (New York: Cornell University Press, 1992)

16. Cambridge Primary Review. Children, their World, their Education: final report and recommendations of the Cambridge Primary Review. October 2009. www.primaryreview.org.uk/publications/final_report.php

17. Schickedanz, Judith. *Much More Than the ABCs: The early stages of reading and writing.* (Washington, DC: NAEYC, 1999)

18. *USA Today.* Average home has more TVs than people. 21 September 2006. www.usatoday.com/life/television/news/2006-09-21-homes-tv_x.htm

19. *The Huffington Post.* Brain development: How much TV should children watch? 5 December 2010. www.huffingtonpost.com/dr-david-perlmutter-md/television-and-the-develo_b_786934.html

20. *The Times.* Children spend half as much time in class as they do looking at a television screen. 21 January 2009. www.timesonline.co.uk/tol/life_and_style/education/article5555797.ece

21. The Joan Ganz Cooney Center. Always connected: the new digital media habits of young children. March 2011. www.joanganzcooneycenter.org/Reports-28.html

22. Mayo, Ed, Nairn, Agnes. *Consumer Kids: How big business is grooming our children for profit.* (London: Constable, 2009)

23. The Joan Ganz Cooney Center. Learning: Is there an app for that? November 2010. www.joanganzcooneycenter.org/Reports-27.html

24. *The New York Times.* The claim: babies tend to look like their fathers. 22 March 2005. www.nytimes.com/2005/03/22/health/22real.html

25. Sue Palmer. Out to play. 2010. www.suepalmer.co.uk/modern_childhood_info_out_to.php

26. *Mail Online.* Calling a child 'naughty' can traumatise them, say experts. 16 October 2006. www.dailymail.co.uk/news/article-410738/Calling-child-naughty-traumatise-say-experts.html

27. *The Times.* Majority of parents admit to smacking children. 20 September 2006. www.timesonline.co.uk/tol/news/uk/article644804.ece

28. *Time Magazine.* The long-term effects of spanking. 3 May 2010. www.time.com/time/magazine/article/0,9171,1983895,00.html#ixzz1YFdQFuWA

29. NHS. Smacking and children's IQ. 25 September 2009. www.nhs.uk/news/2009/09September/Pages/Does-smacking-make-children-stupid.asp

30. *The Telegraph.* Smacked children more successful in later life, study finds. 3 January 2010. www.telegraph.co.uk/health/healthnews/6926823/Smacked-children-more-successful-later-in-life-study-finds.html

31. *news.scotsman.com.* Smack? No, most people ignore naughtiness. 20 October 2008. http://news.scotsman.com/smackingban/Smack-No-most-parents-ignore.4611100.jp

32. *Mail Online.* Mother jailed for BITING her five-year-old son in revenge for hurting his baby sister. 23 September 2008. www.dailymail.co.uk/news/article-1060305/Mother-jailed-BITING-year-old-son-revenge-hurting-baby-sister.html#ixzz1YQLGa5ay

33. healthvisitors.com. Check your child's development at 2 years. 2005–2006. www.healthvisitors.com/parents/development_two_yrs.htm

34. Taylor Nelson Sofres. *Children's Eyesight Study: Vision screening in schools.* (London: Guide Dogs, 2002)

35. Science Daily. Chimpanzees are spontaneously generous after all, study shows. 8 August 2011. www.sciencedaily.com/releases/2011/08/110808152220.htm

36. *New Scientist.* Women may be hardwired to prefer pink. 20 August 2007. www.newscientist.com/article/dn12512-women-may-be-hardwired-to-prefer-pink.html

37. *Scientific American.* The truth about boys and girls. May 2010. www.scientificamerican.com/article.cfm?id=the-truth-about-boys-and-girls

38. *Guardian.* Is Britain becoming a one-child nation? 15 March 2009. www.guardian.co.uk/lifeandstyle/2009/mar/15/single-child-families

39. Newman, Susan. *Parenting an Only Child.* (New York: Doubleday, 1990)

40. *The Times.* Rise of the one and Only Child. 12 January 2008. http://women.timesonline.co.uk/tol/life_and_style/women/body_and_soul/article3171485.ece

41. Aviva. US family shrinks as costs of raising a child reach £270,000. 21 February 2011. www.aviva.co.uk/media-centre/story/9763/uk-family-shrinks-as-cost-of-raising-a-child-reach/

42. CATALYST Consortium. Optimal Birth Spacing. www.coregroup.org/storage/documents/Workingpapers/smrh_OBSI_Overview.pdf

43. American Psychological Association. The joke's in you. November 2007. www.apa.org/monitor/nov07/thejoke.aspx

44. Mayo Clinic. Stress relief from laughter? Yes, no joke. 23 July 2010. www.mayoclinic.com/health/stress-relief/SR00034

Bibliography

Barnet, Ann, Barnet, Richard. *The Youngest Minds: Parenting and genes in the development of intellect and emotion*. (New York: Simon & Schuster, 1998.)

Mayo, Ed, Nairn, Agnes. *Consumer Kids: How big business is grooming our children for profit*. (London: Constable, 2009.)

Morris, Desmond. *Babywatching*. (London: Jonathan Cape, 1991.)

Newman, Susan. *Parenting an Only Child*. (New York: Doubleday, 1990.)

Palmer, Sue. *Toxic Childhood: How the modern world is damaging our children and what we can do about it*. (London: Orion, 2007.)

Schickedanz, Judith. *Much More Than the ABCs: The early stages of reading and writing*. (Washington, DC: NAEYC, 1999.)

Smith, Ruth S., Werner, Emmy E. *Overcoming the Odds: High-risk children from birth to adulthood*. (New York: Cornell University Press, 1992.)

Index

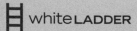
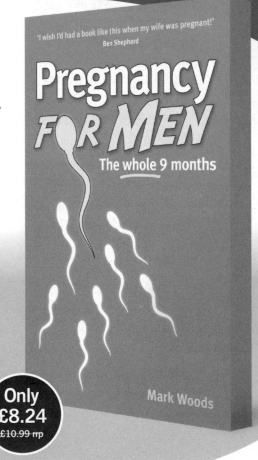

Top tips at your fingertips!

If you're in the midst of your partner's raging pregnancy hormones or knee-deep in nappies then you need *101 Tips*. Offering quick and easy-to-apply advice right when you need it most, these mini books will help you survive the choppy waters of pregnancy and become the best dad in town!

Each book is:

- ✓ Brimming with 101 bite-sized tips
- ✓ Written by the same witty and original author
- ✓ Full of advice from other new dads too

Babies & Toddlers FOR MEN 101 Tips

Mark Woods

Pregnancy FOR MEN 101 Tips

Mark Woods

Only £4.49 £5.99 rrp

Out September 2012

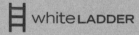
whiteLADDER

Help mum survive and enjoy your baby's first year!

Unlike other boring baby books, *First-time Mum* is a refreshingly honest and friendly guide that new mums can really relate to. With advice on how to change a nappy and cope with sleepless nights to dealing with baby blues and returning to work, *First-time Mum* contains everything a new mum needs to enjoy her new role.

Plus:

✓ Tips from other new mums

✓ Relationship advice

✓ Fun ways to play and bond with your baby

First-time Mum

Surviving and enjoying your baby's first year

Everything that a new mum needs to know

Out July 2012

Hollie Smith

Only £8.24
£10.99 rrp

whiteLADDER

Get 25% off
White Ladder parenting books

White Ladder specialises in providing you with balanced and practical parenting advice. Each book is written by an expert and arms you with the latest information so you can decide what's best for you and your child.

Only £8.24
~~£10.99 rrp~~

Only £4.49
~~£5.99 rrp~~

Only £8.24
~~£10.99 rrp~~

Only £8.24
~~£10.99 rrp~~

Only £7.49
~~£9.99 rrp~~

Only £8.24
~~£10.99 rrp~~

Only £5.24
~~£6.99 rrp~~

Only £7.49
~~£9.99 rrp~~